Bond
No.1 for exam success

Maths

Assessment Papers

9-10 years

Book 2

OXFORD
UNIVERSITY PRESS

Great Clarendon Street, Oxford, OX2 6DP, United Kingdom

Oxford University Press is a department of the University of Oxford.
It furthers the University's objective of excellence in research, scholarship,
and education by publishing worldwide. Oxford is a registered trade mark of
Oxford University Press in the UK and in certain other countries

British Library Cataloguing in Publication Data
Data available

978-0-19-277740-9

10 9 8 7 6 5 4 3

Paper used in the production of this book is a natural, recyclable
product made from wood grown in sustainable forests.
The manufacturing process conforms to the environmental
regulations of the country of origin.

Printed in China

Acknowledgements

The publishers would like to thank the following for permissions to
use copyright material:

Page make-up: OKS Prepress, India
Illustrations: Tech-Set Limited
Cover illustrations: Lo Cole

Although we have made every effort to trace and contact all
copyright holders before publication this has not been possible in all
cases. If notified, the publisher will rectify any errors or omissions at
the earliest opportunity.

Links to third party websites are provided by Oxford in good faith
and for information only. Oxford disclaims any responsibility for
the materials contained in any third party website referenced in
this work.

Before you get started

What is Bond?

This book is part of the Bond Assessment Papers series for maths, which provides **thorough and continuous practice of all the key maths content** from ages five to thirteen. Bond's maths resources are ideal preparation for many different kinds of tests and exams – from SATs to 11+ and other secondary school selection exams.

What does this book cover and how can it be used to prepare for exams?

It covers all the maths that a child of this age would be expected to learn and is fully in line with the National Curriculum for maths and the National Numeracy Strategy. *Maths 9–10 Book 1* and *Book 2* can be used both for general practice and as part of the run up to 11+ exams, Key Stage 2 SATs and other selective exams. One of the key features of Bond Assessment Papers is that each one practises **a wide variety of skills and question types** so that children are always challenged to think – and don't get bored repeating the same question type again and again. We think that variety is the key to effective learning. It helps children 'think on their feet' and cope with the unexpected.

What does the book contain?

- **24 papers** – each one contains 50 questions.
- **Tutorial links throughout** – [B|5] – this icon appears in the margin next to the questions. It indicates links to the relevant section in *How to do … 11+ Maths*, our invaluable subject guide that offers explanations and practice for all core question types.
- **Scoring devices** – there are score boxes in the margins and a Progress Chart on page 72. The chart is a visual and motivating way for children to see how they are doing. It also turns the score into a percentage that can help decide what to do next.
- **Next Steps Planner** – advice on what to do after finishing the papers can be found on the inside back cover.
- **Answers** – located in an easily-removed central pull-out section.

How can you use this book?

One of the great strengths of Bond Assessment Papers is their flexibility. They can be used at home, in school and by tutors to:

- set **timed formal practice** tests – allow about 30 minutes per paper. Reduce the suggested time limit by five minutes to practise working at speed.
- provide **bite-sized chunks** for regular practice.
- highlight **strengths and weaknesses** in the core skills.

- identify **individual needs**.

- set **homework**.

- follow a **complete 11+ preparation strategy** alongside *The Parents' Guide to the 11+ (see below.)*

It is best to start at the beginning and work through the papers in order. Calculators should not be used.

Remind children to check whether each answer needs a unit of measurement before they start a test. If units of measurement are not included in answers that require them, they will lose marks for those questions. To ensure that children can practise including them in their answers, units of measurement have been omitted after the answer rules for some questions.

If you are using the book as part of a careful run-in to the 11+, we suggest that you also have two other essential Bond resources close at hand:

Bond 11+ Maths Handbook: the subject guide that explains all the question types practised in this book. Use the cross-reference icons to find the relevant sections.

The Parents' Guide to the 11+: the step-by-step guide to the whole 11+ experience. It clearly explains the 11+ process, provides guidance on how to assess children, helps you to set complete action plans for practice and explains how you can use the *Maths 9–10 Book 1* and *Book 2* as part of a strategic run-in to the exam.

See the inside front cover for more details of these books.

What does a score mean and how can it be improved?

It is unfortunately impossible to predict how a child will perform when it comes to the 11+ (or similar) exam if they achieve a certain score on any practice book or paper. Success on the day depends on a host of factors, including the scores of the other children sitting the test. However, we can give some guidance on what a score indicates and how to improve it.

If children colour in the Progress Chart on page 72, this will give an idea of present performance in percentage terms. The Next Steps Planner inside the back cover will help you to decide what to do next to help a child progress. It is always valuable to go over wrong answers with children. If they are having trouble with any particular question type, follow the tutorial links to *How to do ... 11+ Maths* for step-by-step explanations and further practice.

Don't forget the website ...!

Visit www.bond11plus.co.uk for lots of advice, information and suggestions on everything to do with Bond, the 11+ and helping children to do their best.

Key words

Some special maths words are used in this book. You will find them **in bold** each time they appear in the papers. These words are explained here.

acute angle an angle that is less than a right angle

factor the factors of a number are numbers that divide into it, for example 1, 2, 4 and 8 are all factors of 8

improper fraction a fraction with the numerator bigger than the denominator

lowest term the simplest you can make a fraction, for example $\frac{4}{10}$ reduced to the lowest term is $\frac{2}{5}$

mean one kind of average. You find the mean by adding all the scores together and dividing by the number of scores, for example the mean of 1, 3 and 8 is 4

median one kind of average, the middle number of a set of numbers after being ordered from lowest to highest, for example the median of 1, 3 and 8 is 3

mixed number a number that contains a whole number and a fraction, for example $5\frac{1}{2}$ is a mixed number

mode one kind of average. The most common number in a set of numbers, for example the mode of 2, 3, 2, 7, 2 is 2

obtuse angle an angle that is more than 90° and not more than 180°

polygon a closed shape with three or more sides

range the difference between the largest and smallest of a set of numbers, for example the range of 1, 2, 5, 3, 6, 8 is 7

reflex angle an angle that is bigger than 180° and less than 360°

vertex, vertices the point where two or more edges or sides in a shape meet

Paper 1

What fraction of the larger shape is the smaller shape?
Work out the **lowest term** fraction for each of these.

1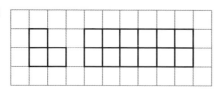

B 10

_____

2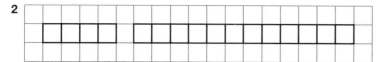

_____ **2**

This is a plan of Jude's ferret cage.

B 12
B 10
B 20

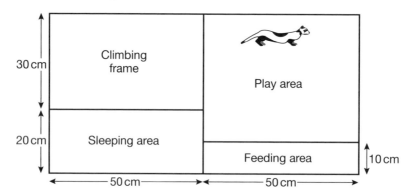

3 What percentage of the cage is used for feeding and playing?   _____ %

4 What is the area of the cage?   _____ cm²

5 What fraction of the cage is taken up by the sleeping area?   _____

6 What fraction of the cage is for feeding?   _____

7 What area is covered by the climbing frame?   _____ cm²

8 Which has the greater area, the play area or the climbing frame?   _____

6

Complete these sequences.

B 7

9–10	26	34	42	____	____	
11–12	____	48	39	30	____	
13–14	____	36	48	____	72	
15–16	36	25	____	____	4	1
17–18	1	2	4	8	____	____

10

Write each of these **mixed numbers** as an **improper fraction**.

19 $2\frac{1}{2} =$ _____

20 $1\frac{2}{3} =$ _____

21 $1\frac{1}{8} =$ _____

22 $2\frac{3}{4} =$ _____

23 $1\frac{4}{5} =$ _____

24 $2\frac{1}{6} =$ _____

What fraction of each shape is grey?

25 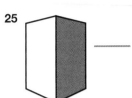 _____

26 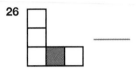 _____

27  _____

28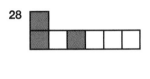

_____

29  _____

30 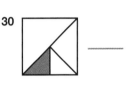 _____

Write down the missing numbers.

31 $206 \times 100 =$ _____

32 $33\,600 \div 100 =$ _____

Look at this line graph of temperatures during one week.

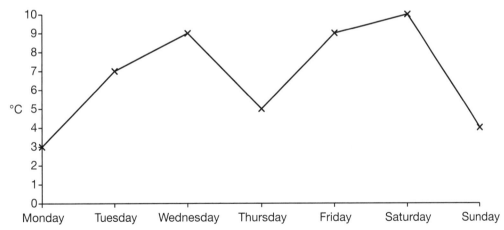

33 On what day was it 5 °C? _____

34 What is the difference between the highest and lowest temperatures? _____°C

35 On which days was the temperature the same? _____ and _____

36 Which was the coldest day? _____

37 Which was the warmest day? _____

38 I think of a number. I double it and then double it again.
I then take away 1.
The answer is 15.
What was the starting number?
_____

Put a sign in each space so that each question is correct.

39–40 (5 ___ 7) ___ 15 = 20

41–42 (8 ___ 4) ___ 12 = 1

43 Write out in words the biggest number that you can make with these digits.

1   9   7   6   8   3

_____

_____

There are two ropes on a canal narrowboat. The one at the front is 18.6 metres long and the one at the rear is 9.8 metres long.

44 What is the difference in length between the two ropes? _____ m

45 If they were joined end to end how long would they be together? _____ m

46–50 Draw the reflections of these shapes in the line of symmetry.

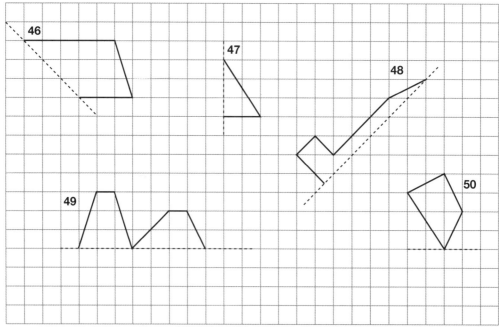

Paper 2

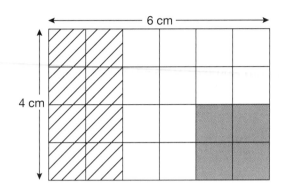

1 What is the area of the whole rectangle?   _____ cm²

2 What is the area of the grey part?   _____ cm²

3 What is the area of the white part?   _____ cm²

Write each of these fractions reduced to its **lowest term**.

4 What fraction of the rectangle is striped?   _____

5 What fraction is grey?   _____

6 What fraction is white?   _____

Look at this map.

Chutney

22.5 km

14.7 km

23.7 km

Brintown

13.8 km

Amberville

28.6 km

20.9 km

Dingleton

7 How far is it from Brintown to Dingleton via Amberville?   _____ km

8 How much further is it from Brintown to Chutney than from Amberville to Dingleton?   _____ km

9 A delivery van goes from Amberville to Brintown, back to Amberville then on to Chutney and then to Dingleton before going back to Amberville.
How far does the van travel? _____ km

10 How far is it from Brintown to Chutney to Dingleton to Amberville? _____ km

11 How far is the round trip from Dingleton to Brintown to Chutney and back to Dingleton without going through Amberville? _____ km

12 How much further is it from Brintown to Dingleton if you go through Amberville than if you go from Brintown to Dingleton direct? _____ km

6

13–16 Circle the **obtuse angles**.

B 17

a   b   c

d   e   f

g   h   i

4

Match one of these words to each of the sentences below.

B 16

CERTAIN   LIKELY   UNLIKELY   IMPOSSIBLE

17 You will kick a ball so hard that it will go into space. _____

18 You won't get a cold this year. _____

19 It will get dark next Thursday night. _____

20 It will rain in the next three weeks. _____

4

Write each of these decimals as a fraction.

B 11

21 0.3 _____

22 0.09 _____

23 2.37 _____

3

24 There are 48 children at the Sports Centre. For every 5 boys there are 7 girls. How many boys are there? _____

25 If a lorry uses 4 litres of diesel every 15 km, how many litres will be used in going 300 km? _____

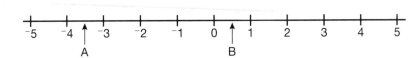

A   B

26 What number is arrow A pointing at? _____

27 What number is arrow B pointing at? _____

What number is halfway between:

28 25 and 29? _____

29 36 and 54? _____

30 27 and 49? _____

Underline the correct answer for each question.

31 $4 \div \frac{1}{2} =$	8	2	$2\frac{1}{2}$	$\frac{1}{4}$	1
32 $\frac{1}{6} + \frac{2}{3} =$	$\frac{3}{9}$	$\frac{2}{18}$	$\frac{2}{6}$	$\frac{5}{6}$	$\frac{3}{3}$
33 What is $\frac{2}{3}$ of 21?	$30\frac{1}{3}$	14	$20\frac{1}{3}$	1.4	41
34 How many $\frac{1}{4}$ in 3?	$\frac{1}{12}$	7	13	1.2	12
35 $2.00 - 0.8 =$	1.02	2.08	1.2	12	1.8
36 What is $\frac{1}{3}$ of 18?	3.6	36	9	6	3

Write down the missing numbers.

37 _____ minutes $\times$ 6 = 2 hours

38 $4^2 =$ _____

39 25p $\times$ _____ = £1.00

40 20p $\times$ _____ = £3.00

Multiply each of these numbers by 100.

41 10.75 _____   **42** 31.6 _____   **43** 10.06 _____

44 1.58 _____   **45** 0.43 _____

46–50 Put each of these numbers in the correct box on the Venn diagram.

21, 15, 25, 30, 22

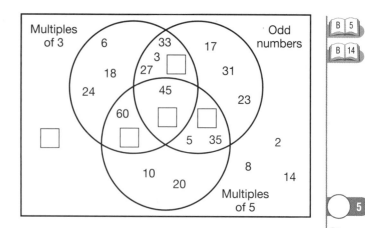

B 5

B 14

5

Paper 3

1 Multiply 32 by 46. _____

B 3

1

Find the total of:

2 £8.57, £21.13 and £4.82. £ _____

3 £16.58, £27.31 and £8.42. £ _____

B 2

2

Here is a chart that shows the number of spectators at seven of Dingleton Cricket Club's matches last summer.

B 14

B 2

4 How many more people watched match 2 than match 3? _____

5 Which match had twice as many spectators as match 3? _____

6 What was the total number of spectators for matches 3, 4 and 5? _____

7 What was the fourth most watched match? _____

8 What was the total number of spectators for matches 1, 2 and 6? _____

9 How many spectators were there altogether at these matches? _____

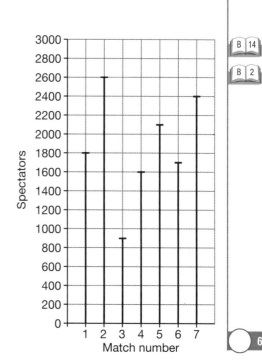

6

10 What number, multiplied by itself, gives 49? _____

11 5 minutes × _____ = half an hour

12 $1\frac{7}{8}$ = _____ eighths

13 $2\frac{2}{3}$ = _____ thirds

14 What is 6 squared? _____

15–17 Write down the numbers that will come out of this machine.

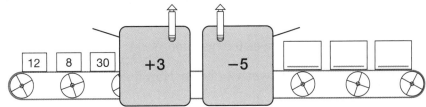

Here is a bar-line chart that shows the colours that a spinner landed on when a group of children did a number of spins.

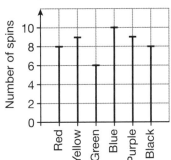
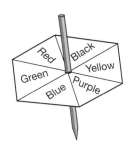

18 How many times did the children spin the spinner altogether? _____

19 How many times did the spinner land on red, yellow or green altogether? _____

20 What is the difference between the total for purple and black and the total for blue and green? _____

21 In its **lowest term**, what fraction of the spins resulted in blue? _____

22 What percentage of the spins were yellow or green? _____ %

Answer these questions using the letters a to h.

a   b   c   d

e   f   g   h

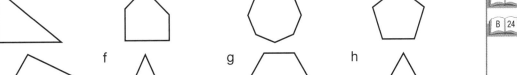

23 Which **polygon** is an equilateral triangle? _____

24 Which **polygon** is an octagon? _____

25 Which **polygon** is a right-angled triangle? _____

26 Which **polygon** is a scalene triangle? _____

27 Which **polygon** is an irregular pentagon? _____

28 Which **polygon** has exactly six lines of symmetry? _____

29 Which triangle has only one line of symmetry? _____

30 Divide a 1.2 m rope into 3 equal pieces. How many centimetres is each piece? _____ cm

31 What number, when divided by 9, gives 6 remainder 3? _____

32 Divide 6 litres of squash equally between 4 people. How much squash does each person get? _____ litres

33 What number, when divided by 8, gives 4 remainder 2? _____

Use these two calculations to answer the questions.

$$\begin{array}{r} 847 \\ -\ 486 \\ \hline 361 \end{array} \qquad \begin{array}{r} 438 \\ +\ 375 \\ \hline 813 \end{array}$$

34 $486 + 361 =$ _____   **35** $813 - 375 =$ _____   **36** $847 - 486 =$ _____

37 $813 - 438 =$ _____   **38** $847 - 361 =$ _____

39 There is 1.5 kg of flour in a bag. It takes one-third of a bag to make a loaf. How many bags are needed to make nine loaves? _____

A coach leaves Penrith at 10:37 and reaches Glasgow at 12:05.

40 How long does the journey take? _____ h _____ min

41 $3^2 =$ _____

42 Multiply 9 by itself. _____

43 $\frac{3}{5} + \frac{2}{5} - \frac{1}{5} =$ _____

44 $\frac{8}{10} - \frac{3}{10} + \frac{2}{10} =$ _____

45 $\frac{8}{100} + \frac{91}{100} =$ _____

46 $\frac{36}{100} + \frac{6}{100} - \frac{3}{100} =$ _____

(10)

Scale: 1 cm represents 1 m. What does each of these lines represent?

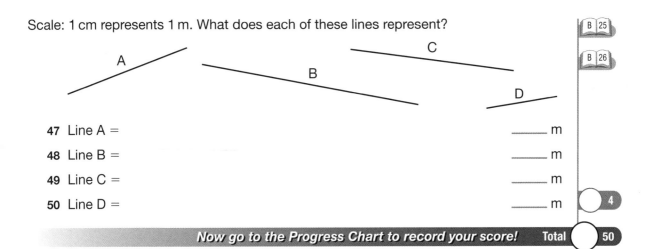

47 Line A = _____ m

48 Line B = _____ m

49 Line C = _____ m

50 Line D = _____ m

4

Now go to the Progress Chart to record your score! **Total** 50

Paper 4

Work out how big the things in this greenhouse are in real life, using a ruler to help you.
Scale: 1 cm represents 1 m.

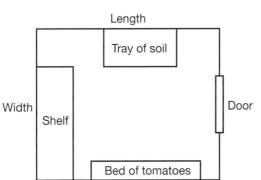

1 How long is the real greenhouse? _____ m

2 How wide is the real greenhouse? _____ m

3–4 How long and wide is the bed of tomatoes in real life?

_____ m long   _____ m wide

5 What is the perimeter of the real shelf? _____ m

6 How wide is the real door? _____ m

7 Which has a bigger perimeter: the bed of tomatoes or the tray of soil?

_____

7

11

Complete these sequences.

8 36 42 ___ 54 60

9 63 72 81 ___ 99

10 49 ___ 63 70 77

11 What multiplication table contains the same sequence of numbers as in question 8? ___

12 What multiplication table contains the same sequence of numbers as in question 9? ___

13 What multiplication table contains the same sequence of numbers as in question 10? ___

Underline the best approximation for:

14 $\frac{1}{2}$ litre: $\frac{1}{4}$ pint $\frac{1}{3}$ pint $\frac{1}{2}$ pint   1 pint $1\frac{1}{2}$ pints

15 2 miles: 1 km   2 km   3 km   4 km   5 km

16 There are 3 boys for every 2 girls watching the high jump on sports day. If there are 10 girls, how many boys are there? ___

17 James has two stickers in his collection for every sticker that William has. If there are 48 stickers altogether, how many does William have? ___

18 Anish squeezes 5 lemons to make $\frac{1}{2}$ litre of real lemonade. How many lemons does Anish have to squeeze to make 4 litres? ___

19–20 The **factors** of 18 are: 1, 2, 3, ___, ___ and 18.

21 The pairs of **factors** of 10 are: 1 and 10, and 2 and ___ .

Multiply each of these numbers by 10.

22 6.5 ___   **23** 10.3 ___   **24** 0.7 ___   **25** 0.93 ___   **26** 0.08 ___

Look at these shapes.

A   B   C

27 Which shape has two square faces? ___

28 Which shape has only one square face? ___

29 Which shape has the least number of edges? ___

30 Which shape has the most rectangular faces? ___

31 What is the sum of the number of faces and edges for shape B? ___

32 How many **vertices** does shape C have? ___

B 7
B 3

6

B 25

2

B 4
B 13
B 13
B 3

3

B 5

3

B 1

5

B 21

6

33 Multiply 300 by 14. _____

34 What number is 25 less than 71? _____

35 What number is 18 more than 67? _____

B3/B2

3

Measure these lines with a ruler.

B 25

A

B

C

D

36 Line A measures _____ mm.   **37** Line B measures _____ mm.

38 Line C measures _____ mm.   **39** Line D measures _____ mm.

4

There are 29 586 people in Bigville.

40 To the nearest 1000 this is approximately _____ people.

41 To the nearest 100 this is approximately _____ people.

42 To the nearest 10 this is approximately _____ people.

B 1

3

B 5

43 The pairs of **factors** of 15 are: 1 and 15, and 3 and _____ .

44 The pairs of **factors** of 21 are: 1 and 21, and 3 and _____ .

45–46 The pairs of **factors** of 32 are: 1 and 32, 4 and _____, and _____ and 16.

4

What are these numbers to the nearest 1000?

47 8498 _____   **48** 11 501 _____   **49** 3600 _____

B 1

3

50 Work out how many times you can subtract 9 from 100. _____

B 3

1

Now go to the Progress Chart to record your score!   Total   50

Paper 5

Complete these sequences.

1–2 24   35   ___   57   ___

3–4 $2\frac{1}{2}$ 4 $5\frac{1}{2}$ ___   ___

5–6 2.95   2.90   ___   2.80   ___

7–8 88   79   ___   61   ___   43

9–10 15   ___   45   60   75   ___

11–12 806   80.6   ___   0.806   ___

B 7
12

A bus driver works five days a week, from 8 o'clock until noon, and from 1.30 p.m. until 5.00 p.m. She has two 15-minute breaks, one in the morning and one in the afternoon.

B2/B3
B4/B27

13 How many hours does she work in a day?   _____ hours

14 How many hours does she work in a week?   _____ hours

2

Look at this line of black and white counters.

○ ○ ● ● ● ○ ○ ● ● ● ○ ○ ● ● ●

B 7

15 What position in the line is the 8th black counter?   _____

16 What colour will the 28th counter be?   _____

2

Write the correct sign, $<$, $>$ or $=$, in each space.

A6/B2
B3/B6

17 7×7 _____ $21 + 29$

18 6^2 _____ $26 + 12$

19 $12 + 18 - 2$ _____ 7×4

3

Write 7546 to the nearest:

B 1

20 1000   _____

21 100   _____

22 10   _____

3
B 1

23 What is the biggest whole number that you can make with these digits?

     5   0   7   1   9   3   _____

24 Write out the answer to question 23.

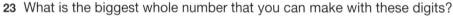

2

How would these times appear on a 24-hour clock?

25 Five past 6 in the morning. _____   **26** 12:15 a.m. _____

27 7:30 p.m. _____   **28** One minute to midnight. _____

29 What number, multiplied by itself, makes 36? _____

30 $7^2 =$ _____

31 What is 8 squared? _____

Write the correct sign, $<$, $>$ or $=$, in each space.

32 6 minutes _____ 350 seconds

33 0.75 m _____ 75 cm

34 12 + 13 _____ 7 + 8 + 9

35 Subtract the product of 8 and 9 from 75. _____

36–39 Plot and label the points
A (1,1), B (2,4), C (4,4) and D (4,2).

40 Join up the points. How many lines
of symmetry does this shape have? _____

Write each of these **improper fractions** as a **mixed number**.

41 $\frac{11}{8}$ _____

42 $\frac{19}{10}$ _____

Two-fifths of the cows on a farm are white. The other 150 are black.

43 How many white cows are there? _____

44 How many cows are there altogether? _____

45 The perimeter of a square is 28 cm. How long is each side? _____ cm

46 Work out how many times you can subtract 23 from 345. _____

Put a number in each space so that each calculation is correct.

47 $479 + \rule{3em}{0.4pt} = 677$

48 $287 - 149 = \rule{3em}{0.4pt}$

49 How many quarters are there in $9\frac{1}{4}$? \rule{3em}{0.4pt}

50 How many days will there be in the first four months of a leap year? \rule{3em}{0.4pt}

Now go to the Progress Chart to record your score! **Total** 50

Paper 6

Seventy-two children have each planted a hyacinth bulb to give as a present. 50% of the bulbs produce pink flowers, $\frac{1}{4}$ purple and the rest white. How many are:

1 pink? \rule{3em}{0.4pt}

2 purple? \rule{3em}{0.4pt}

3 white? \rule{3em}{0.4pt}

Some people were asked whether their favourite holiday destinations were beaches, cities or mountains. Their answers are shown in this Venn diagram.

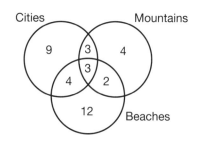

4 How many people were asked? \rule{3em}{0.4pt}

5 How many did not like beaches? \rule{3em}{0.4pt}

6 How many liked both mountains and beaches? \rule{3em}{0.4pt}

7 How many did not like cities? \rule{3em}{0.4pt}

8 How many did not like either mountains or cities? \rule{3em}{0.4pt}

What number is:

9 15 more than 29? \rule{3em}{0.4pt}

10 23 less than 68? \rule{3em}{0.4pt}

Calculate the missing angles.

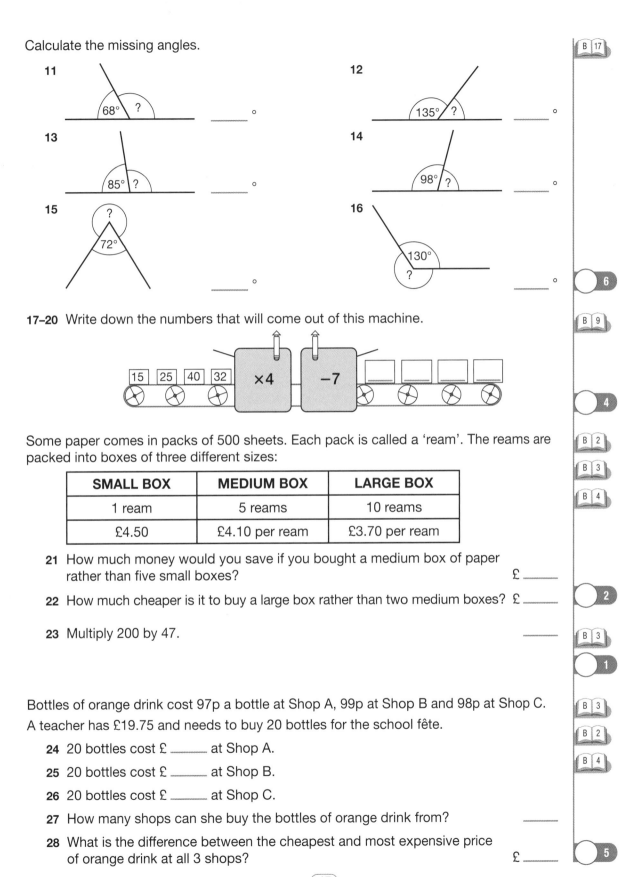

11 68° ? _____ °

12 135° ? _____ °

13 85° ? _____ °

14 98° ? _____ °

15 ? 72° _____ °

16 130° ? _____ °

17–20 Write down the numbers that will come out of this machine.

15 25 40 32 ×4 −7

Some paper comes in packs of 500 sheets. Each pack is called a 'ream'. The reams are packed into boxes of three different sizes:

SMALL BOX	MEDIUM BOX	LARGE BOX
1 ream	5 reams	10 reams
£4.50	£4.10 per ream	£3.70 per ream

21 How much money would you save if you bought a medium box of paper rather than five small boxes? £ _____

22 How much cheaper is it to buy a large box rather than two medium boxes? £ _____

23 Multiply 200 by 47. _____

Bottles of orange drink cost 97p a bottle at Shop A, 99p at Shop B and 98p at Shop C. A teacher has £19.75 and needs to buy 20 bottles for the school fête.

24 20 bottles cost £ _____ at Shop A.

25 20 bottles cost £ _____ at Shop B.

26 20 bottles cost £ _____ at Shop C.

27 How many shops can she buy the bottles of orange drink from? _____

28 What is the difference between the cheapest and most expensive price of orange drink at all 3 shops? £ _____

B 17

6

B 9

4

B 2
B 3
B 4

2

B 3

1

B 3
B 2
B 4

5

Underline the calculations that give a remainder of 3.

29–32 31 ÷ 2   41 ÷ 4   66 ÷ 9   93 ÷ 10

          38 ÷ 7   28 ÷ 6   49 ÷ 5   35 ÷ 8

33 The bus is due to arrive at 11:58 a.m. It is running 13 minutes late. At what time will it arrive? _____

34 Add 24 to 96, then divide your answer by 4. _____

Put a sign in each space so that each question is correct.

35–36 (7 __ 8) __ 6 = 9   **37–38** (15 __ 5) __ 7 = 10

39–40 (7 __ 3) __ 4 = 25

Six children, A to F, were born on the dates shown.

     A 15/4/97   B 23/6/98   C 2/1/98   D 12/9/98   E 29/12/97   F 2/8/97

41 Who has a birthday in August? _____

42 Who has a birthday in June? _____

43 Who has a birthday in April? _____

44 Who is the oldest? _____

45 Who is the youngest? _____

46 Whose birthday is closest to New Year's Day? _____

There are 64 flowers in the garden. One-eighth of them are red.

47 How many red flowers are there? _____

On the pond there are 4 moorhens for every 5 ducks.

48 If there are 20 moorhens, how many ducks are there? _____

On the next pond there are also 4 moorhens for every 5 ducks.

49 If there are 15 ducks, how many moorhens are there? _____

50 How many birds are there altogether on the two ponds? _____

Now go to the Progress Chart to record your score!   Total   50

Paper 7

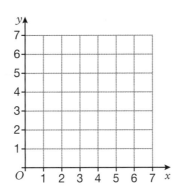

1–6 Plot and label the points A (2,3), B (2,5), C (4,6), D (6,5), E (6,3) and F (4,2).

7 Join up the points. What is the name of this shape? _____

8 How many lines of symmetry does it have? _____

These are the results of a mental mathematics test and a spelling test for ten children.

	Mental mathematics	Spelling
Eric	6	8
Soraya	8	5
Winston	9	8
Ellie	7	5
Francis	10	9
Amy	7	8
Ali	6	7
Daniel	8	4
Patrick	7	8
Amelie	7	6

9 What is the **mode** for mental mathematics? _____

10 What is the **mode** for spelling? _____

11 What is the **range** for mental mathematics? _____

12 What is the **range** for spelling? _____

13 Subtract a quarter of 12 from twice 9. _____

One of the teachers at Dingleton School asked a group of students where they got their lunch, and drew this bar-line graph of the results:

B 14

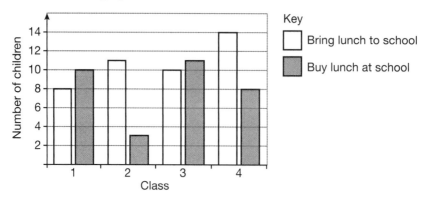

Key
☐ Bring lunch to school
▨ Buy lunch at school

14–21 Complete this table:

Class	Number who bring lunch to school	Number who buy lunch at school
1		
2		
3		
4		

Here is a pie chart that shows what students at Dingleton like best for lunch:

B 14
B 10
B 12
B 3

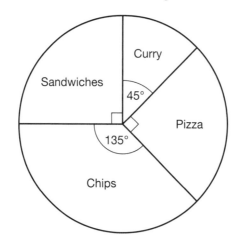

22 What fraction of students like sandwiches best? _____

23 What fraction of students like curry best? _____

24 What percentage of students like pizza best? _____

25 What fraction of students do not like chips best? _____

26 If 100 students like pizza best, how many students are there in the whole school? _____

13

How many halves are there in:

27 14? _____

28 $6\frac{1}{2}$? _____

29 $11\frac{1}{2}$? _____

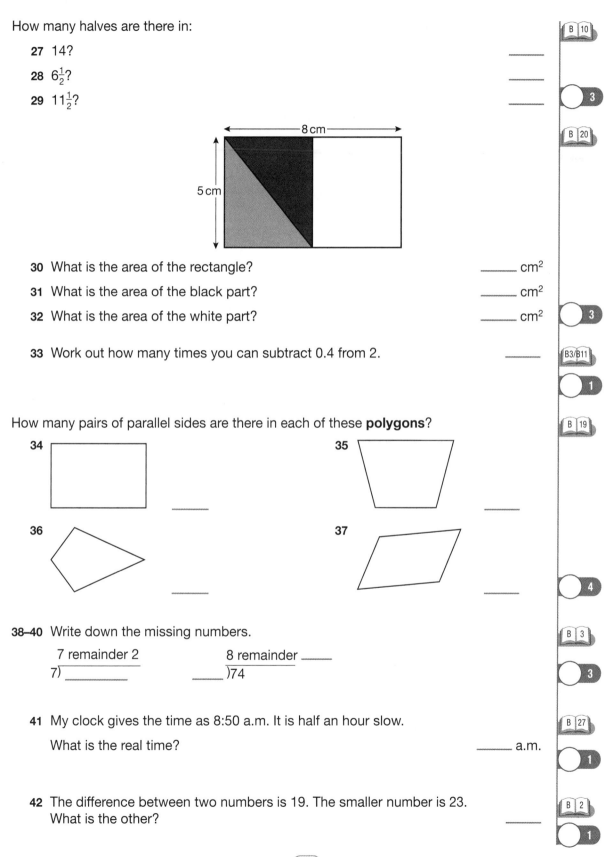

8 cm

5 cm

30 What is the area of the rectangle? _____ cm²

31 What is the area of the black part? _____ cm²

32 What is the area of the white part? _____ cm²

33 Work out how many times you can subtract 0.4 from 2. _____

How many pairs of parallel sides are there in each of these **polygons**?

34 _____

35 _____

36 _____

37 _____

38–40 Write down the missing numbers.

7 remainder 2
7)_____

8 remainder _____
_____)74

41 My clock gives the time as 8:50 a.m. It is half an hour slow.

What is the real time? _____ a.m.

42 The difference between two numbers is 19. The smaller number is 23.
What is the other? _____

B 10

3

B 20

3

B3/B11

1

B 19

4

B 3

3

B 27

1

B 2

1

Siva's watch gains 4 minutes every 12 hours. He put his watch right at 9 a.m. on Friday morning.

B 2
B 27

43 What time will it show at 9 p.m. on Friday? ＿＿ : ＿＿ p.m.

44 What time will it show at 9 a.m. on Saturday? ＿＿ : ＿＿ a.m.

45 If he leaves it, what time will the watch show at 9 a.m. on Sunday morning? ＿＿ : ＿＿ a.m.

46 What time will it show at 9 p.m. on Monday? ＿＿ : ＿＿ p.m.

4

Last July the exchange rates for these currencies were:

B 13

£1 = 2.06 Canadian dollars

£1 = 20 Mexican pesos

£1 = 110 Indian rupees

47 How many Canadian dollars can you get for £100? ＿＿

48 How many British pounds can you get for 550 Indian rupees? ＿＿

49 How many Indian rupees can you get for £50? ＿＿

50 How many Mexican pesos can you get for £30? ＿＿

4

Now go to the Progress Chart to record your score!   **Total**   50

Paper 8

Eric and Jamie have 36 football stickers.

B2/B3
B 4

1–2 Jamie has 4 more than Eric. Eric has ＿＿ and Jamie has ＿＿ .

2

3 How many minutes are there between midnight and 2:31 a.m.? ＿＿

B 27

4 How many weeks are there in 196 days? ＿＿

2

Measure each of the angles in this triangle and say whether they are **acute** or **obtuse**.

B 18
B 17

5–6 A ＿＿°, ＿＿＿

7–8 B ＿＿°, ＿＿＿

9–10 C＿＿°, ＿＿＿

11 What is the sum of all the angles in this triangle? ＿＿°

12 What is the name of this type of triangle? ＿＿＿＿＿

8

22

Here is a line graph that shows the outside temperature in February over 24 hours.

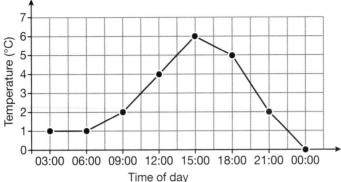

What is the difference in temperature between:

13 9:00 a.m. and midday? _____ °C   **14** 6:00 a.m. and midnight? _____ °C

15 6:00 p.m. and 9:00 p.m.? _____ °C   **16** 9:00 a.m. and 9:00 p.m.? _____ °C

17 The temperature is 8°C. It falls by 11 degrees.
What is the temperature now?   _____ °C

18 The temperature is −4°C. It falls by 5 degrees.
What is the temperature now?   _____ °C

19 The temperature is −6°C. It rises by 9 degrees.
What is the temperature now?   _____ °C

20   8.36
       + 6.98
       _____

21   2.48
       + 3.63
       _____

22   1.27
       + 2.58
       _____

23 Cyril the snake is 6 cm shorter than Cyrus, his older brother. Cyrus is half the
length of a car that is 1.98 m long. How long is Cyril?   _____ cm

Here is a pie chart that shows the ways that 48 children get home from school.

24–25 Which two ways are taken by the same number of children?

_____ and _____

26 How many children walk home?   _____

27 How many children ride bikes?   _____

28 What fraction of children take a bus home?   _____

29 What fraction of children go home in a car?   _____

I roll a dice three times and end up with a total of 11. What three different numbers might I have rolled?

B 5

30 ——— , ——— and ———

31 ——— , ——— and ———

32 ——— , ——— and ———

3

33 What is the smallest number that must be added to 339 to make it exactly divisible by 23? ———

B 5

1

Write each of these decimals as a fraction reduced to its **lowest term**.

B 11

34 0.07 ———   35 6.5 ———   36 2.9 ———

B 10

37 3.25 ———   38 1.75 ———

5

Put a decimal point in each of the following numbers so that the 7 has a value of $\frac{7}{10}$.

B 1

39 1427 ———   40 1742 ———   41 7124 ———

42 1472 ———   43 4217 ———

5

A6/B2

Write the correct sign, $<$, $>$ or $=$, in each space.

B 3

44 $11 - 5 + 4$ ___ $3 + 2 + 7$

B 25

45 5×7 ___ 3×11

B 27

46 $(5 - 2) \times 3$ ___ $(6 + 12) \div 2$

47 0.15 kg ___ 100 g

48 30 m ___ 0.3 km

49 2.5 hours ___ 120 minutes

6

50 What is the perimeter of a rectangle that is 6.4 cm long and 3.2 cm wide?

——— cm

B 20

1

Now go to the Progress Chart to record your score!   Total   50

Paper 9

B 7

1 What will be the colour of the 27th counter in this pattern? _____

B 7

2 What will be the colour of the 40th counter in this pattern? _____

3 What will be the colour of the 50th counter? _____

B25/B6

4 Underline the correct answer.

$\frac{1}{4}$ m² =   1000 cm²   1500 cm²   2000 cm²   2500 cm²   3000 cm²

B2/B3

Put a sign in each space so that each question is correct.

5–6 (8 ___ 5) ___ 7 = 6   **7–8** (12 ___ 6) ___ 5 = 11

9–10 (9 ___ 1) ___ 2 = 16   **11–12** (3 ___ 8) ___ 6 = 4

B 2

13 Subtract seventy-eight from one thousand and twenty. _____

B 20

This is a plan of a garden.

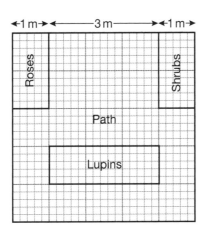

14 What is the area of the rose bed? _____ m²

15 What is the area of the lupin bed? _____ m²

16 What is the area of the path? _____ m²

17 What is the perimeter of the bed of shrubs? _____ m

18 What is the perimeter of the lupin bed? _____ m

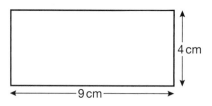

19 What is the area of this rectangle? _____ cm²

20 Underline the dimensions that give the same area as the above rectangle.

5 cm by 5 cm   3 cm by 9 cm   12 cm by 3 cm   8 cm by 3 cm   5 cm by 9 cm

21 Wurzitt & Daughters make Super-Wurzitts. Each Super-Wurzitt is 3 m long. On the conveyor belt there is room for 11 Super-Wurzitts with a space of 1 m between each pair of Super-Wurzitts. How long is the conveyor belt?

_____ m

These triangles have been made on a pinboard using elastic bands.
The pins are 1 cm apart.

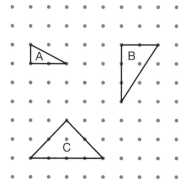

22 What is the area of triangle A? _____ cm²

23 What is the area of triangle B? _____ cm²

24 What is the area of triangle C? _____ cm²

25 Two numbers have a product of 56. One of the numbers is 8.
What is the other number? _____

26 At a fair there was a competition to guess the number of marbles in a jar. There were 400, and the three closest guesses were A: 382, B: 414 and C: 411.
Which was the nearest? _____

The sum of the ages of Annie and Tom is 23.

27 If Tom is 5 years older than Annie, how old is he? _____

28 How old is Annie? _____

This is a regular hexagon. Angle b = Angle c and Angle d = Angle e.

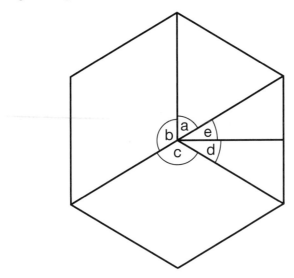

B 17

29 Angle a = _____ °

30 Angle c = _____ °

31 Angle e = _____ °

32 Angle b + c = _____ °   4

Calculate the missing angles.

B 17
B 18

33

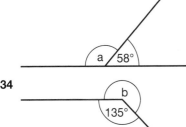

_____ °

34

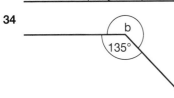

_____ °

35

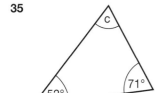

_____ ° 3

36 How many days are there in the autumn months of September, October and November?

B 27

_____ 1

The perimeter of a rectangle is 36 cm. The rectangle is twice as long as it is wide.

37 What is its length? _____ cm

38 What is its width? _____ cm

B 20

2

These are some measurements of water level from a river, which were taken over a period of nine months.

B 14
B 15

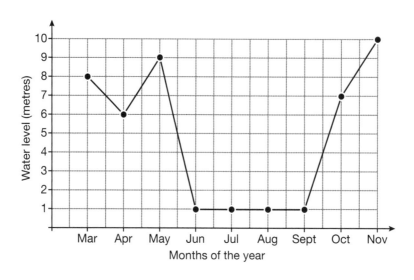

39–41 For which months was the water level higher than the month before? _____ , _____ and _____

42–43 Which months had the lowest water level? _____ to _____

44 Which month was the water level highest? _____

45 The flood level is 10.4 metres. Did the river flood in these nine months? _____

46–47 Between which consecutive months was there the biggest drop in water levels? _____ and _____

48 What is the **range** of water levels over this nine month period? _____ metres

49 What is the **mode** water level over this nine month period? _____ metres

11

50 What is 4567 rounded to the nearest thousand? _____

B 1

1

Paper 10

Here is a bar chart that shows a robin's visits to a bird table.

B 14

B 15

B 10

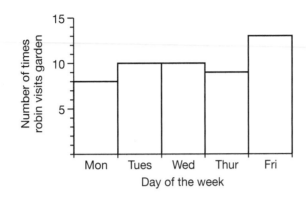

1 On which day did the robin make the most visits? _____

2 What is the total number of visits in the week? _____

3 What is the **mode**? _____

4 What is the **range**? _____

5 What fraction of the week's visits were made on Tuesday and Wednesday? _____

5

I have twice as much money as Anne. She has 46p.

B2/B3

6 How much money do I have? _____ p

7 How much money should I give to Anne if we are to have the same amount each? _____ p

8 How much money would we each have then? _____ p

3

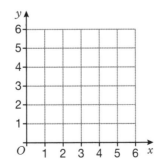

B 23

B 17

9–12 Plot and label the points A (1,1), B (2,3), C (4,3) and D (3,1). Join up the points.

13 How many **acute angles** does this shape have? _____

14 Translate this shape 2 units up and draw its new position.

6

29

There are 320 parrots in the jungle. 20% are red, $\frac{1}{4}$ are blue, 5% are green, $\frac{1}{8}$ are yellow and 10% are purple.

15–16 There are _____ yellow parrots and _____ red ones.

17–18 There are _____ green parrots and _____ purple ones.

19 How many blue parrots are there?   _____

20 How many other parrots are there in the jungle?   _____

21 What is the smallest whole number that you can make with these digits?

8   4   2   7   3   6

_____

22 Write out the answer to question 21 in words.

_____

_____

Place these numbers in order from largest to smallest.

23–27 4.11   4.101   4.111   4.01   4.1   _____, _____, _____, _____, _____

28 One carpet tile is $\frac{3}{4}$ metre long. How many carpet tiles could be fitted into a room 9 metres long?   _____

29 The train left Bigville at 2:35 p.m. and got to Smalltown at 5:25 p.m. How long did the journey take?   _____ h _____ min

30 Tamsin bought three toys that all cost the same. She paid with a £10 note and got £1.03 change. How much did each toy cost?   £ _____

31 How much is left from £5 if Chris buys 4 pens at 85p each?   £ _____

Here is a bar chart that shows the number of days children were absent from school because they were sick.

Key
☐ Term 1
▨ Term 2
■ Term 3

(bar chart: y-axis "Number of days sick" 1–5; x-axis Tom, Radeep, Alex, Ali)

32 Who was sick the most in Term 1?   _____

33 Who was sick the least in Term 3?   _____

34 Who was sick the most in total?   _____

35 Who was sick on two days over the three terms?   _____

36 In what term were the most days taken off sick?   _____

(30)

B 10
B 12
6
B 1
2
B 1
5
B10/B3
1
B 27
1
B2/B3
B 4
2
B 14
B 2
5

A flight took off at 8:15 p.m. and landed at 7:45 a.m.

37 How long did the journey take?   _____ h _____ min

B 17

How many quarters are there in these numbers?

38–41 $3\frac{1}{2}$ = _____ $1\frac{1}{4}$ = _____ $4\frac{1}{4}$ = _____ $2\frac{1}{2}$ = _____

B 10

How many halves are there in these numbers?

42–45 11 = _____ $7\frac{1}{2}$ = _____ $9\frac{1}{2}$ = _____   15 = _____

B 10

8

30 people have registered for football training. Today nine times as many turned up as did not.

46 How many turned up?   _____

47 How many were absent?   _____

B 13
B 3

2

48	431	**49**	156	**50**	7.98
	× 4		× 20		× 6
	_____		_____		_____

B 3

3

Now go to the Progress Chart to record your score!   **Total** 50

Paper 11

Four-ninths of the cars in the car park are estates. The rest are saloons. There are 27 cars altogether.

1 How many estate cars are there?   _____

2 How many saloon cars are there?   _____

B 10

2

Here are some thermometers that show the temperatures at midday over four days in summer.

3 What was Monday's temperature?   _____ °C

4 What was Saturday's temperature?   _____ °C

5 What was Sunday's temperature?   _____ °C

6 What was Friday's temperature?   _____ °C

B 14

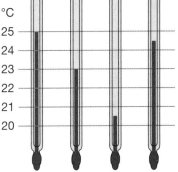

°C
25
24
23
22
21
20

Fri   Sat   Sun   Mon

4

7 Write out 17 451 in words.

_____

8 9.45
  − 3.68
  ‾‾‾‾‾

9 15.16
  + 17.47
  ‾‾‾‾‾

10 644
  × 6.2
  ‾‾‾‾‾

Put a decimal point in each of the following numbers so that the 6 has a value of 6 units.

11 16739 _____

12 93617 _____

13 67139 _____

14 91367 _____

Write down the missing numbers.

15 $6 \times 4 \times$ _____ $= 240$

16 $2 \times 9 \times$ _____ $= 90$

17 $8 \times 2 \times$ _____ $= 48$

18 $5 \times 7 \times$ _____ $= 280$

19 _____ minutes $\times 12 = 2$ hours

Mont Blanc in the Alps is 15 771 feet (4807 m) high. Give its approximate height:

20 to the nearest 1000 m.   _____ m

21 to the nearest 100 m.   _____ m

22 to the nearest 10 m.   _____ m

Jeff bought 100 g of chocolate for £1.40, Karin bought 250 g of chocolate for £3.40 and Omar bought $\frac{1}{2}$ a kilo of chocolate for £6.45.

23 What would a kilogram of Jeff's chocolate cost?   £ _____

24 What would a kilogram of Karin's chocolate cost?   £ _____

25 Who would pay the most for a kilogram of chocolate?   _____

26 Who would pay the least for a kilogram of chocolate?   _____

27–28 The pairs of **factors** of 26 are: 1 and 26, and _____ and _____ .

29–34 The pairs of **factors** of 30 are: 1 and 30, _____ and _____, _____ and _____,

 and _____ and _____ .

35 What is $7^2 - 5^2$?   _____

Carly needs to buy a class a set of 30 rulers and she has exactly £33.
A shatterproof ruler costs £1.09 at Shop A, £1.15 at Shop B and £1.12 at Shop C.

36 30 rulers cost £ _____ at Shop A.

37 30 rulers cost £ _____ at Shop B.

38 30 rulers cost £ _____ at Shop C.

39 Which shop can Carly buy the 30 rulers from?   Shop _____

40 How much change will Carly get?   _____ p

5

41–46 Circle the **polygons** that have a true axis of symmetry.

a   b   c   d

e   f   g   h

6

Complete these sequences.

47–48 2.5   2.75   3   _____   _____

49–50 16   8   4   2   _____   _____

4

Now go to the Progress Chart to record your score!   **Total**   **50**

Paper 12

A class of children did some research on roses in the local park. Here is a Venn diagram of the results.

1 How many roses did the group examine?   _____

2 How many white roses were there?   _____

3 How many scented roses were there?   _____

4 How many white roses were scented?   _____

White roses 7   2   Scented roses 9   3

5 How many roses did they find that had no scent?   _____

6 How many roses were not white and not scented?   _____

6

The coach leaves Exeter for Reading at 06:53. The journey takes 2 hours 34 minutes.

7 What time does the coach arrive at Reading? _____

B 27

Multiply each of these numbers by 100.

8 0.36 _____

9 0.83 _____

10 0.0072 _____

This is a plan of Mr Macgregor's garden.

Scale: 1 cm represents 3 m.

```
┌───────────────┬───────────────────────┐
│               │                       │
│   Flowers     │     Vegetables        │
│               │                       │
├───────────────┴───────────────────────┤
│                 Path                   │
└────────────────────────────────────────┘
←──────────────── 21 m ─────────────────→
```

11 What area of the garden is for vegetables? _____ m²

12 What is the area of the path? _____ m²

13 Mr Macgregor is going to cover his vegetable patch with paving. How many paving stones will he need if they are each 1 m × 1 m? _____

14 He decides to cover the flower bed with paving stones too. How many more paving stones will he need? _____

15 If Mr Macgregor decides to cover the whole garden with his new paving stones, how many more does he need? _____

There are 32 fish in the pond in Gary's garden. For every 3 carp there are 5 goldfish.

16 How many goldfish are there? _____

17 How many fewer carp are there? _____

Write each of these fractions as a decimal.

18 $\frac{43}{100}$ _____

19 $\frac{13}{100}$ _____

20 $\frac{60}{100}$ _____

21 $\frac{7}{100}$ _____

Any answer that requires units of measurement should be marked wrong if the correct units have not been included.

Paper 1 (pages 2–4)

1–2 To write a fraction in its 'lowest terms', divide the numerator (top number) and denominator (bottom number) by the same number, making both numbers as small as possible.

1 $\frac{1}{4}$ The smaller shape covers 3 squares. The larger covers 12 squares. $\frac{3}{12} = \frac{1}{4}$

2 $\frac{1}{3}$ The smaller shape covers 4 squares. The larger covers 12 squares. $\frac{4}{12} = \frac{1}{3}$

3 **50** The length is separated equally into 50cm + 50cm (100cm total). 50cm out of 100cm = $\frac{50}{100}$, which is the same as 50%.

4–8 To find the area of a rectangle, multiply the length by the width.

4 **5000** 50cm + 50 cm = 100cm (length); 20cm + 30cm = 50cm (width), so $100 \times 50 = 5000\text{cm}^2$.

5 $\frac{1}{5}$ Area of cage is $100 \times 50 = 5000\text{cm}^2$ and sleeping area is $20 \times 50 = 1000\text{cm}^2$. This means 1000cm out of 5000cm $\left(\frac{1000}{5000}\right)$ is taken up by the sleeping area. This fraction in its lowest terms is $\frac{1}{5}$.

6 $\frac{1}{10}$ The total area is $100\,\text{cm} \times 50\,\text{cm} = 5000\ \text{cm}^2$ and the feeding area is $50\,\text{cm} \times 10\,\text{cm} = 500\ \text{cm}^2$; This means 500 out of 5000 $\left(\frac{500}{5000}\right)$ is for feeding. $\frac{500}{5000}$ in its lowest terms is $\frac{1}{10}$.

7 **1500** $30\,\text{cm} \times 50\,\text{cm} = 1500\,\text{cm}^2$

8 **Play area** Area of climbing frame = 1500cm^2 ($30\,\text{cm} \times 50\,\text{cm}$); area of play area = 2000cm^2 ($40\,\text{cm} \times 50\,\text{cm}$).

9–18 First work out the sequence between the numbers by looking at the numbers adjacent to one another: they will have either been added to, subtracted from, multiplied or divided. Then use the same rule to find the missing number or numbers.

9–10 **50, 58** The sequence is to add 8; 42 + 8 = 50; 50 + 8 = 58.

11–12 **57, 21** The sequence is to subtract 9; 57 – 9 = 48; 30 – 9 = 21.

13–14 **24, 60** The sequence is to add 12; 24 + 12 = 36; 48 + 12 = 60.

15–16 **16, 9** The sequence is to subtract 11, then 9, then 7, then 5, then 3; 25 – 9 = 16; 16 – 7 = 9.

17–18 **16, 32** The sequence is to multiply by 2; 8 × 2 = 16; 16 × 2 = 32.

19–24 A mixed number is a whole number and fraction written together, e.g. $2\frac{1}{2}$ or $3\frac{1}{4}$; an improper fraction is a fraction that has a numerator larger than the denominator, e.g. $\frac{5}{8}$ or $\frac{4}{3}$.

19 $\frac{5}{2}$ There are 2 halves in 1, so there are 4 halves in 2 $\left(\frac{4}{2}\right)$. Add this to the $\frac{1}{2}$ in the mixed number to make $\frac{5}{2} \left(\frac{4}{2} + \frac{1}{2} = \frac{5}{2}\right)$.

20 $\frac{5}{3}$ There are 3 thirds in 1 $\left(\frac{3}{3}\right)$. Add this to the $\frac{2}{3}$ to make $\frac{5}{3} \left(\frac{3}{3} + \frac{2}{3} = \frac{5}{3}\right)$.

21 $\frac{9}{8}$ There are 8 eighths in 1 $\left(\frac{8}{8}\right)$. Add this to the $\frac{1}{8}$ to make $\frac{9}{8} \left(\frac{8}{8} + \frac{1}{8} = \frac{9}{8}\right)$.

22 $\frac{11}{4}$ There are 4 quarters in 1, so there are 8 quarters in 2 $\left(\frac{8}{4}\right)$. Add this to the $\frac{3}{4}$ to make $\frac{11}{4} \left(\frac{8}{4} + \frac{3}{4} = \frac{11}{4}\right)$.

23 $\frac{9}{5}$ There are 5 fifths in 1 $\left(\frac{5}{5}\right)$. Add this to the $\frac{4}{5}$ to make $\frac{9}{5} \left(\frac{5}{5} + \frac{4}{5} = \frac{9}{5}\right)$.

24 $\frac{13}{6}$ There are 6 sixths in 1, so there are 12 sixths in 2 $\left(\frac{12}{2}\right)$. Add this to the $\frac{1}{6}$ to make $\frac{13}{6}$ $\left(\frac{12}{6} + \frac{1}{6} = \frac{13}{6}\right)$.

25 $\frac{1}{2}$ The hexagon is halved.

26 $\frac{1}{5}$ There are 5 squares, 1 of which is shaded.

27 $\frac{2}{5}$ Imagine the pentagon divided into 5 equal triangles, 2 of which are shaded.

28 $\frac{3}{7}$ There are 7 squares, 3 of which are shaded.

29 $\frac{2}{5}$ There are 5 equal bands, 2 of which are shaded.

30 $\frac{1}{8}$ Imagine the square divided into 8 identical triangles, 1 of which is shaded.

31–32 Refer to Paper 2 Q41–45 multiply or divide by a power of 10.

31 **20,600**

10,000s	1000s	100s	10s	ones
		2	0	6
2	0	6	0	0

32 **336**

10,000s	1000s	100s	10s	ones
3	3	6	0	0
		3	3	6

33 **Thursday** The vertical axis shows temperature. The horizontal axis shows days of the week.

34 **7** The highest point on the graph is 10 °C and the lowest is 3 °C; 10 °C – 3 °C = 7 °C.

35 **Wednesday and Friday** It was 9 °C on Wednesday and on Friday. It can help to put a ruler or set square on the graph.

36 **Monday** The lowest temperature was 3 °C.

37 **Saturday** The highest temperature was 10 °C.

38 **4** Work in reverse. Add 1 to 15, halve the answer and halve it again to find the final answer.

39–42 Try different operations to see which of them works. Follow the rules of BIDMAS (Brackets, Indices, Division, Multiplication, Addition, Subtraction) and complete the equation in the brackets first.

39–40 **×, −** $(5 \times 7) - 15 = 35 - 15 = 20$

41–42 **+, ÷** $(8 + 4) \div 12 = 12 \div 12 = 1$

43 **Nine hundred and eighty-seven thousand, six hundred and thirty-one** Order the numbers from largest to smallest then put them in a place-value grid.

1,00,000s	10,000s	1000s	100s	10s	ones
9	8	7	6	3	1

44 **8.8** $18.6 - 9.8 = 8.8$; check by adding $(8.8 + 9.8 = 18.6)$.

45 **28.4** $18.6 + 9.8 = 28.4$; check by subtracting $(28.4 - 9.8 = 18.6)$.

46–50

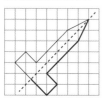
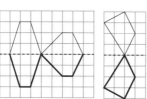

Paper 2 (pages 5–8)

1 **24** Refer to Paper 1 Q4–8 on area. $6 \times 4 = 24$; count the squares to check.

2 **4** 4 of the squares are grey.

3 **12** 12 of the squares are white.

4–6 Refer to Paper 1 Q1–2 on reducing a fraction to its lowest terms.

4 $\frac{1}{3}$ 8 of the 24 squares are striped; $\frac{8}{24} = \frac{1}{3}$.

5 $\frac{1}{6}$ 4 of the 24 squares are grey; $\frac{4}{24} = \frac{1}{6}$.

6 $\frac{1}{2}$ 12 of the 24 squares are white; $\frac{12}{24} = \frac{1}{2}$.

7 **34.7** Brintown to Amberville is 13.8 km; Amberville to Dingleton is 20.9 km; $13.8 + 20.9 = 34.7$.

8 **1.6** Brinton to Chutney is 22.5 km; Amberville to Dingleton is 20.9 km: $22.5 \text{ km} - 20.9 \text{ km} = 1.6 \text{ km}$.

9 **86.9** Amberville to Brinton and back is 13.8 km + 13.8 km = 27.6 km; Amberville to Chutney is 14.7 km (27.6 km + 14.7 km = 42.3 km); on to Dingleton is 23.7 km (42.3 km + 23.7 km = 66.0 km); from Dingleton to Amberville is 20.9 km (66.0 km + 20.9 km = 86.9 km).

10 **67.1** The sum of 3 distances: 22.5 km + 23.7 km + 20.9 km = 67.1 km.

11 **74.8** This is the sum of the distances in a complete circuit: 28.6 km + 22.5 km + 23.7 km = 74.8 km.

12 **6.1** Brinton to Dingleton via Ambleton is 34.7 km (13.8 km + 20.9 km); Brinton direct to Dingleton is 28.6 km; 34.7 km − 28.6 km = 6.1 km.

13–16 **b, c, e, g** Use a protractor. An obtuse angle is greater than 90°, so use the larger numbers on the protractor.

17–20 These questions are about probability (how likely something is to happen). Only things that will definitely happen can be labelled as certain.

17 **Impossible**   18 **Unlikely**

19 **Certain**   20 **Likely**

21–23 Write the numbers in a place value grid:

ones	•	$\frac{1}{10}$	$\frac{1}{100}$
0	•	3	
0	•	0	9
2	•	3	7

21 $\frac{3}{10}$ 0.3 has 3 tenths.

22 $\frac{9}{100}$ 0.09 has 0 tenths and 9 hundredths.

23 $2\frac{37}{100}$ or $\frac{237}{100}$ 2.37 has 2 wholes and 37 hundredths, or 237 hundredths.

24 **20** To solve a ratio, add up the ratio numbers $(5 + 7 = 12)$. Then divide this number into the number of children $(48 \div 12 = 4)$. Finally, multiply this number by the individual ratios $(5 \times 4 \text{ boys} = 20 \text{ boys})$.

25 **80** 300 km ÷ 15 km = 20, so the lorry needs 20 lots of 4 litres; $20 \times 4 = 80$.

$$\begin{array}{r} 0\ \ 2\ \ 0 \\ \hline 15\ |\ 3\ \ ^30\ \ 0 \end{array}$$

26 **−3.5 or −3$\frac{1}{2}$**   27 **0.5 or $\frac{1}{2}$**

28–30 To find a number halfway between, add the two numbers together and then divide by 2.

28 **27** $25 + 29 = 54$; $54 \div 2 = 27$

29 **45** $36 + 54 = 90$; $90 \div 2 = 45$

30 **38** $27 + 49 = 76$; $76 \div 2 = 38$

31 **8** 4 is the same as $\frac{4}{1}$, so the sum becomes $\frac{4}{1} \div \frac{1}{2}$. To divide the fractions, swap the numbers in the last fraction and change ÷ to ×: $\frac{4}{1} \times \frac{2}{1}$. Multiply the numerators together, then the denominators together: $\frac{4}{1} \times \frac{2}{1} = \frac{8}{1}$. $\frac{8}{1}$ is the same as 8.

A2

32 $\frac{5}{6}$ Change the fractions so that they have the same denominator. In this case, $\frac{2}{3}$ can be changed into $\frac{4}{6}$, so the sum becomes: $\frac{4}{6} + \frac{1}{6} = \frac{5}{6}$.

33 14 $\frac{1}{3}$ of 21 is 7 so $\frac{2}{3}$ is 2 × 7 = 14.

34 12 There are 4 quarters in 1; 3 × 4 = 12.

35 1.20 Write the numbers as a column subtraction, ensuring the decimal points are aligned. Add a zero in any gaps to make sure both numbers have the same amount of digits.

```
  ¹2 . ¹0  0
−   0 . 8  0
─────────────
    1 . 2  0
```

36 6 To find $\frac{1}{3}$, divide by 3: 18 ÷ 3 = 6

37 20 There are 60 minutes in an hour; 120 minutes in 2 hours; 120 ÷ 6 = 20.

38 16 4 squared (4^2) means 4 × 4.

39 4 25p + 25p + 25p + 25p = 100p (£1) or 4 × 25p = 100p (£1).

40 15 5 × 20p coins make £1; 3 × 5 = 15.

41–45 To multiply or divide by a power of 10, place the numbers in a decimal grid with hundreds, tens, ones, tenths, hundredths, thousandths, etc. Multiply a number by moving it to the left: count the zeros in the number to find how many places to move it. To multiply by 10 move it one place to the left; by 100 move it two places; by 1000 move it three places, and so on. Add a zero in the ones, tens, hundreds, etc, if they are left empty. To divide a number, count the zeros and move it to the right, adding a zero before the decimal point and in any gaps after it if need be.

41 1075

1000s	100s	10s	ones	.	$\frac{1}{10}$	$\frac{1}{100}$
		1	0	.	7	5
1	0	7	5	.		

42 3160

1000s	100s	10s	ones	.	$\frac{1}{10}$
		3	1	.	6
3	1	6	0	.	

43 1006

1000s	100s	10s	ones	.	$\frac{1}{10}$	$\frac{1}{100}$
		1	0	.	0	6
1	0	0	6	.		

44 158

100s	10s	ones	.	$\frac{1}{10}$	$\frac{1}{100}$
		1	.	5	8
1	5	8	.		

45 43

10s	ones	.	$\frac{1}{10}$	$\frac{1}{100}$
	0	.	4	3
4	3	.		

46–50

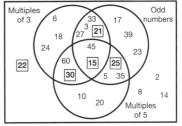

A multiple is the answer when two numbers are multiplied together.
21 is an odd number and a multiple of 3 (but not a multiple of 5).
15 is an odd number, a multiple of 3 and a multiple of 5.
25 is an odd number and a multiple of 5 (but not a multiple of 3).
30 a multiple of 3 and of 5 (but not an odd number).
22 is not an odd number, nor a multiple of 3 or of 5.

Paper 3 (pages 8–11)

1 1472 Use long multiplication to complete the:

```
        3 2
  ×     4 6
  ─────────
      1 9 2
+ 1 2 8 0
  ─────────
  1 4 7 2
        ₁
```

```
        4 6
  ×     3 2
  ─────────
        9 2
          ₁
+ 1 3 8 0
      ₁
  ─────────
  1 4 7 2
        ₁
```

2 34.52 Add the pounds (£8 + £21 + £4 = £33), then the pence (57p + 13p + 82p = 152 pence, which is £1.52) and add these together (£33 + £1.52 = £34.52), or set out as a column addition sum, making sure the decimal points are aligned:

```
      8 . 5 7
    2 1 . 1 3
+     4 . 8 2
  ───────────
    3 4 . 5 2
    ₁ ₁   ₁
```

3 52.31 £16.58 + £27.31 + £8.42 = £52.31

4 1700 2600 – 900; note that the number of spectators (on the vertical axis) goes up in steps of 200.

5 1 900 × 2 = 1800, so Match 1.

6 4600 900 + 1600 + 2100 = 4600

7 **1** Start with the most watched and count down on the graph.

8 **6100** 1800 + 2600 + 1700 = 6100

9 **13,100** Add the totals: as they contain no 10s or ones, ignore the zeros and add the remaining numbers: 18 + 26 + 9 + 16 + 21 + 17 + 24 = 131. Then put the zeros back on: 13,100.

10 **7** 7 × 7 = 49

11 **6** 30 minutes ÷ 5 = 6.

12 **15** There are 8 eighths in 1 whole; 8 eighths + 7 eighths = 15 eighths $\left(\frac{8}{8} + \frac{7}{8} = \frac{15}{8}\right)$.

13 **8** There are 3 thirds in 1 whole, therefore 6 thirds in 2; 6 thirds + 2 thirds = 8 thirds $\left(\frac{6}{3} + \frac{2}{3} = \frac{8}{3}\right)$.

14 **36** 6 squared means 6 × 6.

15–17 **10, 6, 28** Work from left to right taking each number in turn; 12 + 3 − 5 = 10; 8 + 3 − 5 = 6; 30 + 3 − 5 = 28.

18 **50** Add together how many times each colour has been recorded: 8 + 9 + 6 + 10 + 9 + 8 = 50

19 **23** 8 + 9 + 6 = 23

20 **1** Total of purple and black = 17; total of blue and green = 16. 17 − 16 = 1.

21 $\frac{1}{5}$ Of the fifty spins 10 were blue; $\frac{10}{50} = \frac{1}{5}$. Refer to Paper 1 Q1–2 on reducing a fraction to its lowest terms.

22 **30** Total of number of spins = 50. 9 yellow spins + 6 green spins = 15; $\frac{15}{50} = \frac{3}{10}$. To write this as a percentage, change it to an equivalent fraction with a denominator of 100 (multiply both numbers by 10 so $\frac{3}{10}$ becomes $\frac{30}{100}$). The numerator is then the same number as the percentage: 30%.

23–29 A polygon is a shape with at least 3 sides and 3 angles.

23 **h** An equilateral triangle has equal angles (60°) and all sides the same length.

24 **c** An octagon has 8 sides.

25 **a** A right-angled triangle has a 90° angle.

26 **e** A scalene triangle has 3 different angles and sides of different lengths.

27 **b** A pentagon has 5 sides. An irregular shape has sides that are different lengths.

28 **g** A regular hexagon has 6 equal angles and 6 sides the same length, therefore 6 lines of symmetry as well.

29 **f** If a shape has a line of symmetry, the shapes on either side of the line will be identical.

30 **40** Change 1.2m into 120cm, then divide by 3 (120 ÷ 3 = 40cm) or 1.2 m ÷ 3 = 0.4 m (40 cm)

```
    0 . 4
 3 | 1 . ¹2
```

31 **57** 9 × 6 = 54; 54 + 3 = 57

32 **1½ or 1.5** 6 litres = 6000ml: 6000 ÷ 4 = 1500ml; 1500ml = 1½ litres. An alternate method is: 6 ÷ 4 = 1½ 1.5 litres.

```
    1 . 5
 4 | 6 . ²0
```

33 **34** 8 × 4 = 32 + 2 = 34

34–38 These are number families, where the 3 numbers shown can be added and subtracted in any order and the numbers remain unchanged. The first (847 − 486 = 361) can be changed to any of the following: 847 − 361 = 486, 486 + 361 = 847 or 361 + 486 = 847. The second (438 + 375 = 813) can be changed in the same way.

34 **847**   35 **438**   36 **361**

37 **375**   38 **486**

39 **3** 1.5kg = 1500g; divide 1500 by 3 to find $\frac{1}{3}$: 1500 ÷ 3 = 500g. 500g × 9 loaves = 4500g. 4500g ÷ 1500g (one bag) = 3 bags.

40 **1 hr 28 mins** 10:37 + 23 minutes = 11:00. 11:00 to 12:05 = 1hr 5mins. 1hr 5mins + 23mins = 1hr 28mins.

41 **9** 3² = 3 × 3 = 9   42 **81** 9 × 9 = 81

43–46 To add and subtract fractions with the same denominator, simply add the numerators.

43 $\frac{4}{5} + \frac{3}{5} = \frac{5}{5}, \frac{5}{5} - \frac{1}{5} = \frac{4}{5}$

44 $\frac{7}{10} - \frac{8}{10} = \frac{3}{10}, \frac{5}{10} + \frac{2}{10} = \frac{7}{10}$

45 $\frac{99}{100} - \frac{8}{100} + \frac{91}{100} = \frac{99}{100}$

46 $\frac{39}{100} - \frac{36}{100} + \frac{6}{100} = \frac{42}{100}, \frac{42}{100} - \frac{3}{100} = \frac{39}{100}$

47–50 Measure each line with a ruler. 1 cm represents 1 m, so 2 cm represents 2 m, and so on.

47 **3½ or 3.5**   48 **6**

49 **4½ or 4.5**   50 **2**

Paper 4 (pages 11–13)

1–7 Refer to Paper 3 Q47–50 on using a scale where 1 cm represents 1 m.

1 **5**   2 **4**

3–4 **3m long, ½ or 0.5m wide**

5 **8** Perimeter is the distance all around the edge; 3 + 3 + 1 + 1 = 8.

6 **1½ or 1.5**

7 **Bed of tomatoes** The perimeter of the bed of tomatoes is 3 + 3 + 0.5 + 0.5 = 7 and the perimeter of the tray of soil is 2 + 2 + 1 + 1 = 6.

8–10 Refer to Paper 1 Q9–18 on sequences.

8 **48** The sequence is to add 6; 42 + 6 = 48.

9 **90** The sequence is to add 9; 81 + 9 = 90.

10 **56** The sequence is to add 7; 49 + 7 = 56.

11 **6**   12 **9**   13 **7**

14–15 These questions are about equivalent Metric and Imperial measures used in everyday life.

14 **1 pint** 1 litre = 1.75 pints; 1.75 ÷ 2 = 0.875 litres; 0.875 rounded to the nearest whole number = 1, so the answer is 1 pint.

15 **3 km** 5 miles = 8km, so 1m = 1.6km. 1.6 × 2 = 3.2 miles; 3.2 rounded to the nearest whole number = 3, so the answer is 3km.

16–18 Refer to Paper 2 Q24 on ratio.

16 **15** $5 × 2 = 10$, so $5 × 3 = 15$ boys.

17 **16** The ratio is 2 : 1; 2 + 1 = 3. 48 ÷ 3 = 16.

18 **40** If 5 lemons make $\frac{1}{2}$ litre, 10 lemons make 1 litre; 10 × 4 = 40.

19–21 A factor divides into a number without leaving a remainder. A factor pair is two numbers that are multiplied together to make a number.

19–20 **6, 9** $6 × 3 = 18$ and $9 × 2 = 18$

21 **5** $2 × 5 = 10$

22–26 Refer to Paper 2 Q41–45 on how to multiply decimal numbers by powers of 10.

22 **65**   23 **103**   24 **7**

25 **9.3**   26 **0.8**

27–30 A face is a flat surface of a 3D shape, an edge is where two faces meet and a vertex is a corner where three or more faces or edges meet.

27 **B** The top and bottom faces are squares of different dimensions.

28 **C** The base of this pyramid is square.

29 **C** C has 8 edges, whereas A and B each have 12.

30 **A** Each face on A is rectangular, whereas B has two and C has one (a square is a type of rectangle).

31 **18** 6 faces + 12 edges = 18.

32 **5** "Vertices" is the plural of "vertex".

33 **4200** $3 × 14 = 42$; $42 × 100 = 4200$

34 **46** Round 71 up to 75 by adding 4: 75 – 25 = 50. Then subtract the 4 you have added: 50 – 4 = 46

35 **85** Round 18 up to 20 by adding 2: 67 + 20 = 87. Then subtract the 2 you have added: 87 – 2 = 85

36–39 10mm = 1cm

36 **5**   37 **60**

38 **45**   39 **20**

40–42 When rounding a number to the nearest power of 10, look at the number in the next place value column. For example, when rounding a number to the nearest 100, look at the number in the tens column. If it is 4 or below, leave the number in the hundreds column unchanged. If it is 5 or above, raise the number in the hundreds column by 1.

40 **30,000** The 5 in 29,586 rounds up, which in turn rounds the 9 up to 0 and the 2 up to 3, to make 30,000.

41 **29,600** The 8 in 29,586 rounds up to 29,600.

42 **29,590** The 6 in 29,586 rounds up to 29,590.

43–46 Refer to Paper 4 Q19–21 on factors.

43 **5** $3 × 5 = 15$ 44 **7** $3 × 7 = 21$

45–46 **8, 2** $4 × 8 = 32$, $2 × 16 = 32$

47–49 Refer to Paper 4 Q40–42 on rounding.

47 **8,000** The 4 in 8498 rounds down to 8000.

48 **12,000** The 5 in 11 501 rounds up to 12,000.

49 **4,000** The 6 in 3600 rounds up to 4000.

50 **11** Divide 100 by 9: 100 ÷ 9 = 11 remainder 1 (9 × 11 = 99).

Paper 5 (pages 14–16)

1–12 Refer to Paper 1 Q9–18 on sequences.

1–2 **46, 68** The sequence is to add 11.

3–4 **7, $8\frac{1}{2}$** The sequence is to add $1\frac{1}{2}$.

5–6 **2.85, 2.75** The sequence is to subtract 0.05.

7–8 **70, 52** The sequence is to subtract 9.

9–10 **30, 90** The sequence is to add 15.

11–12 **8.06, 0.0806** The sequence is to divide by 10. Refer to Paper 2 Q41–45 on how to divide numbers by powers of 10.

13 **7** 8.00 a.m. to 12.00 p.m. is 4 hours; 1.30 p.m. to 5.00 p.m. is $3\frac{1}{2}$ hours; the total of two 15-minute breaks is $\frac{1}{2}$ hour; $4 + 3\frac{1}{2} = 7\frac{1}{2}$ hrs; $7\frac{1}{2}$ hrs $– \frac{1}{2}$ hr break = 7hrs

14 **35** Multiply the number of hours she works in a day by 5 (7 × 5 = 35).

15 **14** Identify the eighth black counter, then count all the counters from the left.

16 **Black** The counters are in patterns of 5 (2 white and then 3 black). 5 sets of 5 is 25. Count on 3 more to find the 28th counter.

17 **<** $7 × 7 = 49$; $21 + 29 = 50$. 49 is less than 50.

18 **<** $6^2 = 6 × 6$, which is 36; $26 + 12 = 38$. 36 is less than 38.

19 **=** $12 + 18 – 2 = 28$, $7 × 4 = 28$

20–22 Refer to Paper 4 Q40–42 on rounding.

20 **8000** The 5 in 7546 rounds up to 8000.

21 **7500** The 4 in 7546 rounds down to 7500.

22 **7550** The 6 in 7546 rounds up to 7550.

23 **975,310** Order the digits from largest to smallest.

24 **Nine hundred and seventy-five thousand, three hundred and ten** Refer to Paper 1 Q43 on writing large numbers.

25–28 On a digital, 24-hour clock, morning starts from 00.00 hours to 11:59, afternoon starts at 12.00 and then nights ends at 23:59. 00:01 – 11:59 is a.m.; 12:00 – 23:59 is p.m. To change from analogue time to digital time, add 12 to the hour from 1pm onwards; to change from digital to analogue, subtract 12 from 13:00 onwards.

25 **06:05**   26 **00:15**

27 **19:30**

28 **23:59**

29 **6** $6 \times 6 = 36$

30 **49** $7^2 = 7 \times 7 = 49$

31 **64** Eight squared means $8 \times 8 = 64$.

32 **>** 6 minutes = 6×60 seconds = 360 seconds, which is greater than 350 seconds.

33 **=** $0.75\,m = \frac{3}{4}\,m$ and $75\,cm = \frac{3}{4}\,m$

34 **>** $12 + 13 = 25$ and $7 + 8 + 9 = 24$

35 **3** The product is found when multiplying 2 numbers together: $8 \times 9 = 72$; $75 - 72 = 3$

36–39 When plotting coordinates on a grid, use the rule "along the corridor and up the stairs" to remember to go horizontal, then vertical.

40 **1** If a shape has a line of symmetry, the shapes on either side of the line will be identical.

41–42 Refer to Paper 1 Q19-24 on Improper Fractions and Mixed Numbers.

41 **$1\frac{3}{8}$** There are 8 eighths in 1 whole $\left(\frac{8}{8}\right)$: $\frac{8}{8} + \frac{3}{8} = \frac{11}{8}$, so $1\frac{3}{8}$

42 **$1\frac{9}{10}$** There are 10 tenths in 1 whole $\left(\frac{10}{10}\right)$: $\frac{10}{10} + \frac{9}{10}$ $= \frac{19}{10}$, so $1\frac{9}{10}$.

43–44 $\frac{2}{5}$ are white, so $\frac{3}{5}$ must be black. $\frac{3}{5}$ is 150, so $\frac{1}{5}$ is 50 cows.

43 **100** $\frac{2}{5}$ is $2 \times 50 = 100$

44 **250** $\frac{5}{5}$ is $5 \times 50 = 250$

45 **7** A square has four sides of equal length: $28 \div 4 = 7$.

46 **15** To solve this try estimation $(23 \times 10 = 230)$ which leaves 115 $(345 - 230 = 115)$; $23 \times 5 = 115$; $10 + 5 = 15)$ or use long division:

```
        0  1  5
  2 3 | 3  4  5
     -  2  3
        1  1  5
        1  1  5
              0
```

47 **198** $479 + 200 = 679$; this is 2 more than needed, therefore the answer is 2 less than 200.

48 **138** $287 - 150 = 137$ but 150 is 1 too many; $137 + 1$ gives the answer.

49 **37** There are 4 quarters in 1 whole; so there are 36 quarters in 9; 36 quarters + 1 quarter = 37 quarters.

50 **121** January has 31 days, February (leap year) has 29 days, March has 31 days, April has 30 days. $31 + 29 + 31 + 30 = 121$.

Paper 6 (pages 16–18)

1 **36** $50\% = \frac{1}{2}$; $72 \div 2 = 36$

2 **18** $72 \div 4 = 18$

3 **18** $1 - \frac{1}{2} - \frac{1}{4} = \frac{1}{4}$, $\frac{1}{4} = 18$

4 **37** Add all the numbers in the Venn diagram.

5 **16** Add the numbers outside the circle for "Beaches"; $9 + 4 + 3 = 16$.

6 **5** Add the numbers in the overlap of the circles for "Mountains" and "Beaches"; $3 + 2 = 5$.

7 **18** Add the numbers outside the circle for "Cities"; $12 + 2 + 4 = 18$.

8 **12** Find the number not in either of the circles for "Mountains" or "Cities".

9 **44** This can be done mentally by rounding 29 up to 30 and then adding $30 + 15$, which is 45; subtract the 1 that was added when rounding to get the answer of 44.

10 **45** Round 23 down to 20 by subtracting 3 and subtract 20 from 68 $(68 - 20 = 48)$; then subtract the 3 that was removed when rounding to get the answer of 45.

11–14 $180°$ is a straight angle.

11 **112** $180 - 68 = 112$

12 **45** $180 - 135 = 45$

13 **95** $180 - 85 = 95$

14 **82** $180 - 98 = 82$

15–16 There are $360°$ in a whole turn around a point.

15 **288** $360 - 72 = 288$

16 **230** $360 - 130 = 230$

17 **53** $15 \times 4 = 60$; $60 - 7 = 53$

18 **93** $25 \times 4 = 100$; $100 - 7 = 93$

19 **153** $40 \times 4 = 160$; $160 - 7 = 153$

20 **121** $32 \times 4 = 128$; $128 - 7 = 121$

21 **2** 5 small boxes = $5 \times £4.50 = £22.50$. A medium box contains 5 reams at £4.10 each; $5 \times £4.10 = £20.50$. $£22.50 - £20.50 = £2.00$.

22 **4** A large box contains 10 reams at £3.70 each; $10 \times £3.70 = £37.00$. 2 medium boxes contain 10 reams at £4.10 each: $10 \times £4.10 = £41.00$. $£41.00 - £37.00 = £4.00$.

23 **9400** $47 \times 100 = 4700$; double 4700 = 9400

24 **19.40** $97p \times 10 = £9.70$; $£9.70 \times 2 = £19.40$

25 **19.80** $99p \times 10 = £9.90$; $£9.90 \times 2 = £19.80$

26 **19.60** $98p \times 10 = £9.80$; $£9.80 \times 2 = £19.60$

27 **2** The price at shop B is too high.

28 **0.40** Shop A is cheapest and shop B is most expensive; $£19.80 - £19.40 = £0.40$.

29–32 Use your multiplication tables to solve these questions.

29 **66 ÷ 9** $9 \times 7 = 63$, so $66 \div 9 = 7\ r\ 3$

30 **93 ÷ 10** $10 \times 9 = 90$, so $93 \div 10 = 9\ r\ 3$

31 **38 ÷ 7** $7 \times 5 = 35$, so $38 \div 7 = 5\ r\ 3$

32 **35 ÷ 8** $8 \times 4 = 32$, so $35 \div 8 = 4\ r\ 3$

33 **12.11 p.m.** Add 2 minutes to reach noon, then add 11 minutes.

34 **30** $96 + 4 = 100$; $100 + 20 = 120$; $120 \div 4 = 30$

35–40 Try different operations on the numbers in the brackets first.

35–36 **+, −** $(7 + 8) − 6 = 15 − 6 = 9$

37–38 **÷, +** $(15 ÷ 5) + 7 = 3 + 7 = 10$

39–40 **×, +** $(7 × 3) + 4 = 21 + 4 = 25$

41–46 The convention in the UK is to set out dates as day/month/year.

41 **F** August is the eighth month.

42 **B** June is the sixth month.

43 **A** April is the fourth month.

44 **A** Look for the earliest month in the dates showing 97 (1997).

45 **D** Look for the latest month in the dates showing 98 (1998).

46 **C** 2nd January is the day after New Year's Day.

47 **8** $64 ÷ 8 = 8$

48–50 Refer to Paper 2 Q24 on ratio.

48 **25** $20 = 5$ groups of 4, therefore there are 5 groups of 5 ducks; $5 × 5 = 25$.

49 **12** $15 = 3$ groups of 5, therefore there are 3 groups of 4 moorhens; $3 × 4 = 12$.

50 **72** On the first pond there are 20 moorhens and 25 ducks; on the second pond there are 12 moorhens and 15 ducks; $20 + 25 + 12 + 15 = 72$.

Paper 7 (pages 19–22)

1–6 Refer to Paper 5 Q36–39 on co-ordinates.

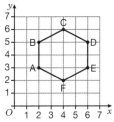

7 **(Irregular) Hexagon** Hexagons have 6 sides. Regular hexagons have all sides of equal length. Irregular hexagons have sides which are not all of equal length.

8 **2** If a shape has a line of symmetry, the shape on either side of the line will be identical.

9–12 The mode is the most common number. The range is the difference between the highest and lowest number.

9 **7** 7 occurs most often.

10 **8** 8 occurs most often.

11 **4** $10 − 6 = 4$ **12** **5** $9 − 4 = 5$

13 **15** $\frac{1}{4} × 12 = 3$; $2 × 9 = 18$; $18 − 3 = 15$

14–21 Read the figures from the bar line graph to complete the table.

Class	Number who bring lunch to school	Number who buy lunch at school
1	8	10
2	11	3
3	10	11
4	14	8

22–25 Refer to Paper 1 Q1–2 on reducing a fraction to its lowest terms.

22 $\frac{1}{4}$ **or** $\frac{90}{360}$ The "sandwiches" segment is a right angle, which is 90°. Angles around the central point of the circle will always be 360°, so the fraction is $\frac{90}{360}$. $\frac{90}{360}$ can be reduced to $\frac{1}{4}$ in its lowest terms.

23 $\frac{1}{8}$ **or** $\frac{45}{360}$ The "curry" segment has an angle of 45°. $\frac{45}{360}$ can be reduced to $\frac{1}{8}$ in its lowest terms.

24 **25%** The "pizza" segment has an angle of 90° which is $\frac{1}{4}$. $\frac{1}{4}$ is equivalent to 25%.

25 $\frac{5}{8}$ **or** $\frac{225}{360}$ The "chips" segment has an angle of 135°; $360° − 135° = 225°$. $\frac{225}{360}$ can be reduced to $\frac{5}{8}$ in its lowest terms.

26 **400** The "pizza" segment is a quarter of the circle; 100 students are a quarter of the school; $100 × 4 = 400$

27 **28** There are 2 halves in 1, so there are 28 halves in 14.

28 **13** There are 12 halves in 6; 12 halves + 1 half = 13 halves.

29 **23** There are 22 halves in 11; 22 halves + 1 half = 23 halves.

30 **40** Refer to Paper 1 Q4–8 on area. $5 × 8 = 40cm^2$.

31 **10** To find the area of a triangle, multiply the base by the height and divide the answer by 2. The triangle is half the length of the 8cm (4cm) and 5cm high, so $4 × 5 = 20$ and $20 ÷ 2 = 10cm^2$.

32 **20** The white area is $\frac{1}{2}$ of the rectangle; $40 ÷ 2 = 20cm^2$.

33 **5** Keep adding 0.4 until 2.0 is reached: $0.4 + 0.4 + 0.4 + 0.4 + 0.4 = 2$

34–37 Parallel lines are two lines that are always the same distance apart, they never meet or cross. Parallel sides will do the same.

34 **2** Opposite sides of a rectangle are parallel.

35 **1** A trapezium has 1 pair of parallel sides, in this case the top and bottom.

36 **None or 0** There are no parallel sides in a kite.

37 **2** Opposite sides of a parallelogram are parallel.

38–40 Use your multiplication tables to complete the calculation.

38 **51** $7 × 7 = 49$; $49 + 2 = 51$

39–40 **9, 2** $7 × 7 = 49 + 2 = 51$; $74. ÷ 8 = 9 r 2$

$$
\begin{array}{r} 7 \text{ remainder } 2 \\ 7\overline{\smash{)}5\ 1} \end{array}
\qquad
\begin{array}{r} 8 \text{ remainder } 2 \\ 9\overline{\smash{)}7\ 4} \end{array}
$$

41 **9:20** $8:50 + 10$ minutes $= 9:00$; 30 mins − 10 mins = 20 mins, so add on the remaining 20 mins: $9:00 + 20$ mins $= 9:20$.

42 **42** Add 19 and 23 together to find the missing number: $19 + 23 = 42$

43 **9.04** After 12 hours the watch will be 4 minutes fast.

44 **9.08** Two lots of 12 hours have passed, so two lots of 4 minutes need to be added (8 mins).

45 **9.16** Four lots of 12 hours have passed, so four lots of 4 minutes need to be added (16 mins).

46 **9.28** Seven lots of 12 hours have passed, so seven lots of 4 minutes need to be added (28 mins).

47–50 Refer to Paper 2 Q41–45 on how to multiply and divide numbers by powers of 10.

47 **206** If $2.06 is equal to £1, multiply both numbers by 100 to find out how many Canadian dollars there are for £100 (2.06 × 100 = 206).

48 **5** If 110 rupees is equal to £1, divide 550 by 110 to find how many pounds there are (550 ÷ 110 = 5).

49 **5500** If 110 rupees is equal to £1, multiply both numbers by 50 to find out how many Indian rupees there are for £50 (5 × 110 = 550, so 50 × 110 = 5500).

50 **600** If 20 pesos is equal to £1, multiply both numbers by 30 to find out how many Mexican pesos there are for £30 (3 x 20 = 60, so 30 × 20 = 600).

Paper 8 (pages 22–24)

1–2 **16, 20** Divide 36 by 2 to find a middle number of 18. Jamie has 4 more, so divide 4 in half to get 2. Subtract 2 from 18 to get Eric's amount (16) and add 2 to 18 to get Jamie's amount (20).

3 **151** There are 60 minutes in an hour; 2 × 60 = 120; 120 + 31 = 151.

4 **28** There are 7 days in one week, so divide by 7: 196 ÷ 7 = 28

5–10 Use a protractor. An acute angle is less than 90°, so use the smaller numbers on the protractor. Refer to Paper 2 Q13–16 Obtuse angles.

5–6 **32, Acute**   7–8 **116, Obtuse**
9–10 **32, Acute**   11 **180**

12 **Isosceles** An isosceles triangle has 2 equal angles and 2 equal sides.

13–16 The horizontal axis shows time and the vertical axis shows temperature.

13 **2** The temperature at 9.00 a.m. (09:00) is 2 °C and at midday (12:00) it is 4 °C.

14 **1** The temperature at 6.00 a.m. (06:00) is 1 °C and at midnight (00:00) it is 0 °C.

15 **3** The temperature at 6.00 p.m. (18:00) is 5 °C. and at 9.00 p.m. (21:00) it is 2 °C.

16 **0** The temperature at 9.00 a.m. (09:00) is 2 °C and at 9.00 p.m. (21:00) it is 2 °C.

17 **−3** 8 − 11 = −3

18 **−9** (−4) − 5 = −9   19 **3** (−6) + 9 = 3

20–22 Refer to Paper 3 Q2 on adding decimal numbers using column addition.

20 **15.34**

```
    8 . 3  6
  + 6 . 9  8
  ───────────
  1 5 . 3  4
      ₁   ₁
```

21 **6.11**

```
    2 . 4  8
  + 3 . 6  3
  ───────────
    6 . 1  1
      ₁   ₁
```

22 **3.85**

```
    1 . 2  7
  + 2 . 5  8
  ───────────
    3 . 8  5
        ₁
```

23 **93** Divide 1.98 by 2 to find the length of Cyrus (198 ÷ 2 = 0.99m or 99cm); subtract 6cm from this to find the length of Cyril (99 − 6 = 93cm).

24–25 **Walking and car** These are the 2 segments of the same size.

26 **8** Examine the pie chart. The "walking" segment is $\frac{1}{6}$ of the circle; 48 ÷ 6 = 8.

27 **12** A quarter of the children ride bikes; 48 ÷ 4 = 12.

28 $\frac{1}{3}$ The "bus" segment is $\frac{1}{3}$ of the circle.

29 $\frac{1}{6}$ The "car" segment is $\frac{1}{6}$ of the circle.

30–31 There are many possibilities. If your solution adds up to 11 then it is correct.

30 **e.g. 1, 4, 6**   31 **e.g. 2, 3, 6**
32 **e.g. 2, 4, 5**
33 **6** 339 ÷ 23 = 14 r 17; 17 + 6 = 23

34–38 Refer to Paper 2 Q21–23 on using a place value grid to convert decimals into fractions and Paper 1 Q1–2 on reducing a fraction to its lowest terms.

34 $\frac{7}{100}$ 0.07 has no tenths and 7 hundredths.

35 $6\frac{1}{2}$ 0.5 is a half so 6.5 is $6\frac{1}{2}$.

36 $2\frac{9}{10}$ 2.9 has 2 wholes and 9 tenths.

37 $3\frac{1}{4}$ 0.25 is $\frac{25}{100}$ which can be reduced to $\frac{1}{4}$, so 3.25 is $3\frac{1}{4}$.

38 $1\frac{3}{4}$ 0.75 is $\frac{75}{100}$ which can be reduced to $\frac{3}{4}$, so 1.75 is $1\frac{3}{4}$.

39–43 **7** Tenths are always the digit on the right of a decimal point in a number therefore the decimal will be before the 7 in the number. (Refer to the place value grids shown on Paper 2 Q41–45.)

39 **142.7**   41 **0.7124**   43 **421.7**
40 **1.742**   42 **14.72**
44 **<** 11 − 5 = 6; 6 + 4 = 10 and 3 + 2 + 7 = 12
45 **>** 5 × 7 = 35 and 3 × 11 = 33

46 = (5 − 2) × 3 = 3 × 3, = 9 and (6 + 12)
÷ 2 = 18 ÷ 2, = 9
47 > 0.15 kg is 150 g.
48 < 0.3 km is 300 m.
49 > 2.5 hours is 150 minutes.
50 **19.2** Refer to Paper 4 Q5 on perimeter.
6.4 + 6.4 + 3.2 + 3.2 = 19.2.

Paper 9 (pages 25–28)

1 **White** The counters are in patterns of 8
(3 white and then 5 black); 3 sets of 8 is 24.
Count on 3 more to find the 27th counter.
2 **Grey** The counters are in patterns of 7
(2 white, 2 black and 3 grey); 5 sets of 7 is 35.
Count on 5 more to find the 40th counter.
3 **White** 7 sets of 7 counters is 49. Count on
1 more to find the 50th counter.
4 **2500 cm²** 1 m² is 1 m × 1 m; 1 m is the
equivalent of 100 cm, so 100 cm × 100 cm
= 10 000 cm² and $\frac{1}{4}$ of 10 000 = 2500 cm².
5–12 Try different operations and follow the rules
of BIDMAS by working out the sum in the
brackets first.
5–6 **+, −** (8 + 5) − 7 = 13 − 7 which is 6
7–8 **−, +** (12 − 6) + 5 = 6 + 5 which is 11
9–10 **−, ×** (9 − 1) × 2 = 8 × 2 which is 16
11–12 **×, ÷** (3 × 8) ÷ 6 = 24 ÷ 6 which is 4
13 **942** Refer to Paper 2 Q35 on column
subtraction.
14–19 Refer to Paper 1 Q4–8 on area of a rectangle
and Paper 4 Q5 on perimeter. Each large
square on the plan represents 1 m × 1 m.
14 **2** 1 m × 2 m = 2 m²
15 **3** 1 m × 3 m = 3 m²
16 **18** Total area is: 5 × 5 = 25 m². Subtract the
area of the roses, lupins and shrubs from 25:
25 − 2 − 3 − 2 = 18 m²
17 **6** The shrub bed is a rectangle measuring 2 m
by 1 m; 2 + 2 + 1 + 1 = 6 m.
18 **8** The lupin bed is a rectangle measuring 3 m
by 1 m; 3 + 3 + 1 + 1 = 8 m.
19 **36** 9 cm × 4 cm = 36 cm².
20 **12 cm by 3 cm** Use your knowledge of
multiplication tables to find the answer.
21 **38** It can sometimes help to draw a picture.
There are 11 Super-Wurzitts making a length
of 33 m. If they are placed in pairs, there will
be one row of 5 and another of 6, as shown
in the diagram. There are 5 spaces of 1 m
between them; 33 m + 5 m = 38 m.

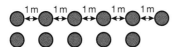

22–24 Refer to Paper 7 Q31 on area of a triangle.
22 **1** 2 × 1 = 2; 2 ÷ 2 = 1 cm²
23 **3** 2 × 3 = 6; 6 ÷ 2 = 3 cm²
24 **4** 4 × 2 = 8; 8 ÷ 2 = 4 cm²
25 **7** Refer to Paper 5 Q35 on finding the product.
8 × 7 = 56.
26 **C** A is 18 less, B is 14 more and C is 11 more.
27–28 Subtract the 5 from 23 to get 18. Divide 18
by 2 to find the number halfway in between,
which will be Annie's age: 18 ÷ 2 = 9. Add
the 5 back on to find Tom's age: 9 + 5 = 14.
Check by adding their ages together:
9 + 14 = 23.
27 **4**   **28** **9**
29–35 Angles around a point always add up to
360°; angles in a triangle always add up
to 180°; angles on a straight angle always add
up to 180°.
29 **60** Draw a line from the central point of the
shape to each corner: a hexagon will be
separated into 6 triangles. This means there
will be 6 angles around the central point:
360° ÷ 6 = 60°, therefore angle a = 60°.
30 **120** Angle c is twice the size of angle a:
60° + 60° = 120°.
31 **30** Angle e is half the size of angle a:
60° ÷ 2 = 30°.
32 **240** Angle b is the same as angle c:
120° + 120° = 240°
33 **122** 180 − 58 = 122.
34 **225** 360 − 135 = 225.
35 **57** 52 + 71 = 123; 180 − 123 = 57.
36 **91** There are 30 days in September
and November and 31 in October;
30 + 30 + 31 = 91.
37–38 **12, 6** The perimeter of a rectangle can be
found by adding up the 2 lengths and the
2 widths. If the total perimeter is 36 cm, divide
this by 2 to get the total of one length and one
width: 36 ÷ 2 = 18. The rectangle has a length
twice as long as it is wide, so this is in a ratio
of 2:1 (Refer to Paper 2 Q24 on ratio). 2 + 1
= 3, so divide 18 by 3 (18 ÷ 3 = 6). Use the
ratio of 2:1 to find the measurements: the
length is 12 (2 × 6) and the width is 6 (1 × 6).
39–49 The month is shown on the horizontal axis and
the water level is shown on the vertical axis.
39–41 **May, October and November** Look for
sections on the graph where the line slopes
upwards.
42–43 **June to September** The water level in these
months was 1 m.
44 **November** Look for the highest point on the
graph.
45 **No** The highest water level was 10 m, which is
less than 10.4 m.

46–47 **May and June** In May the water level was 9 m and in June it was 1 m.

48–49 Refer to Paper 7 Q9–12 on mode and range.

48 **9**   **49** **1**

50 **5000** Refer to Paper 4 Q40–42 on rounding; the 5 in 4567 rounds up to 5000.

Paper 10 (pages 29–31)

1–5 Read the vertical scale to find the number of visits for each day of the week. Line a ruler up with the top of each line/to help read the measurements.

1 **Friday** Look for the highest bar on the chart.

2 **50** Add the number of visits on each of the days; 8 + 10 + 10 + 9 + 13 = 50.

3–4 Refer to Paper 7 Q 9–12 on mode and range.

3 **10** 10 visits occur most often.

4 **5** 13 – 8 = 5.

5 $\frac{2}{5}$ The total visits in the week was 50. Tuesday and Wednesday account for 20 of these; $\frac{20}{50} = \frac{2}{5}$. Refer to Paper 1 Q1–2 on reducing a fraction to its lowest terms.

6 **92** 2 × 46 = 92

7 **23** Find the total amount of money: 46 + 92 = 138; 138 ÷ 2 = 69, so each need to have 69p; 92 – 69 = 23.

8 **69**

9–13 Refer to Paper 5 Q36–39 on plotting coordinates and Paper 8 Q5–10 on angles.

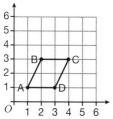

13 **2** A parallelogram has 2 acute angles and 2 obtuse angles.

14 To translate a shape, move it without rotating or resizing it; the whole shape moves 2 squares up.

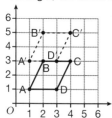

15–20 To find a percentage of a number, first of all find 10% by dividing by 10, e.g. 10% of 450 = 45. To find 20%, multiply the answer by 2, to find 30% multiply by 3, and so on. 5% is half of 10%. To find a fraction of a number, divide

the number by the denominator in the fraction, e.g. to find $\frac{1}{4}$ divide by 4, to find $\frac{1}{5}$ divide by 5 and so on.

15–16 **40, 64** 320 ÷ 8 = 40 yellow parrots. 10% of 320 is 32, so 20% is 32 × 2 = 64 red parrots.

17–18 **16, 32** 10% of 320 is 32 purple parrots; and 5% is half of 32 (32 ÷ 2 = 16) green parrots.

19 **80** 320 ÷ 4 = 80 blue parrots

20 **88** 320 – (40 + 64 + 16 + 32 + 80) = 320 – 232 = 88 other parrots

21 **234,678** Order the digits from smallest to largest.

22 **Two hundred and thirty-four thousand, six hundred and seventy-eight** Refer to Paper 1 Q43.

23–27 **4.111, 4.11, 4.101, 4.1, 4.01** Place the numbers in a grid, ensuring the decimal points are aligned. Add a zero in any gaps so all numbers have the same amount of digits. Look for the largest number in the first column: if they are all the same go onto the next column, and so on.

4	·	1	1	0
4	·	1	0	1
4	·	1	1	1
4	·	0	1	0
4	·	1	0	0

28 **12** Refer to Paper 2 Q31 on dividing fractions. $9 ÷ \frac{3}{4}$ is the same as $\frac{9}{1} × \frac{4}{3}$ which = $\frac{36}{3}$; $\frac{3}{3} = 1$ whole, $\frac{6}{3} = 2$ wholes and so on, therefore $\frac{36}{3}$ = 12 wholes.

29 **2 h 50 m** Looking at the times, 2:35 and 5:25, you can see the journey time is 10 minutes less than 3 hours. You can also count up to 5:25 in minutes and hours: 2:35 to 3:00 is 25 minutes; 3:00 to 5:00 is 2hrs; 5:00 to 5:25 is 25 minutes. 2 hrs + 25 mins + 25 mins = 2hrs 50 mins.

30 **2.99** £10 – £1.03 = £8.97; £8.97 ÷ 3 = £2.99 Refer to Paper 3 Q30-32 on how to divide into decimal numbers.

31 **1.60** 4 × 85p = £3.40; £5 – £3.40 = £1.60

32–36 The horizontal axis shows the names of the children. The vertical axis shows the number of days off sick. The white bars represent Term 1, the grey bars represent Term 2 and the black bars represent Term 3.

32 **Ali** Compare the white bars representing Term 1: Ali has the highest bar.

33 **Radeep** Radeep has no black bar, which represents days off in Term 3: this means he had 0 which is the least.

34 **Alex** Add the number of days for Term 1, 2

and 3 for each child: Alex had the most days off (9 days).

35 **Radeep** 1 day in Term 1 and 1 in Term 2.

36 **Term 1** Add the number of days shown by the white bar for Term 1, then the grey bar for Term 2 and the black bar for Term 3. The highest amount is 12 days in Term 1.

37 **11 h 30 min** If the plane had arrived at 7.15 a.m. it would have taken exactly 11 hours but it took 30 minutes longer. An alternative way is to count on to 7:45 am: 8.15 pm to 9 pm is 45 mins; 9 pm to midnight is 3 hrs; midnight to 7 am is 7 hrs; 7 am to 7:45 am is 45 minutes. Add minutes and hours together separately: 45 mins + 45 mins = 90 mins ($1\frac{1}{2}$ hrs); 3 hrs + 7 hrs = 10 hrs. 10 hrs + $1\frac{1}{2}$ hrs = $11\frac{1}{2}$ hrs.

38 **14** There are 4 quarters in 1 whole, so 12 quarters in 3; there are 2 quarters in $\frac{1}{2}$; 12 quarters + 2 quarters = 14 quarters.

39 **5** There are 4 quarters in 1, so 4 quarters + 1 quarter = 5 quarters.

40 **17** There are 16 quarters in 4, so 16 quarters + 1 quarter = 17 quarters.

41 **10** There are 8 quarters in 2 and 2 quarters in $\frac{1}{2}$; 8 quarters + 2 quarters = 10 quarters.

42 **22** There are 2 halves in 1 whole, so 22 halves in 11.

43 **15** There are 14 halves in 7 so 14 halves + 1 half = 15 halves.

44 **19** There are 18 halves in 9 so 18 halves + 1 half = 19 halves.

45 **30** There are 2 halves in 1 whole, so 30 halves in 15.

46–47 The number of people who turned up is in the 9 times table and is less than 30: this means it could be 9, 18 or 27. If it were 9, only 1 person would not have attended. If it were 18, 2 people would not have attended so it must be 27. Check by adding the numbers together (27 + 3 = 30) and that one number is nine times the other (9 × 3 = 27).

46 **27**   47 **3**

48 **1724**

```
      4  3  1
  ×         4
  1  7  2  4
     1     1
```

49 **3120**   50 **47.88**

```
      1  5  6
  ×      2  0
  3  1  2  0
     1     1
```

```
      7  .  9  8
  ×            6
  4  7  .  8  8
        5     4
```

1 **12** Divide 27 by 9 to find $\frac{1}{9}$ (27 ÷ 9 = 3) then multiply this by 4 to find $\frac{4}{9}$ (3 × 4 = 12), therefore $\frac{4}{9}$ of 27 = 12.

2 **15** 27 – 12 = 15

3–6 The vertical scale goes up in increments of 1 °C, so if the temperature is shown as halfway between two numbers (e.g. 24 and 25), use 0.5 or $\frac{1}{2}$.

3 **24.5 or $24\frac{1}{2}$**   4 **23**

5 **20.5 or $20\frac{1}{2}$**   6 **25**

7 **Seventeen thousand, four hundred and fifty-one.** Refer to Paper 1 Q43 on how to use place value to write large numbers.

8 **5.77**   9 **32.63**

```
  8 9  .  13 4   1 5
  −   3  .  6    8
      5  .  7    7
```

```
      1  5  .  1  6
  +   1  7  .  4  7
      3  2  .  6  3
            1     1
```

10 **3992.8** Remove the decimal point and complete the calculation as normal. Replace the decimal point in the answer: there is 1 decimal point in the sum, so there will be 1 decimal point in the answer (39928 becomes 3992.8).

```
         6  4  4
  ×         6  2
      1  2  8  8
      2  2
   3  8  6  4  0
         1
   3  9  9  2  8
```

An alternative method is: 644 × 62 = 39 928, so 644 × 6.2 = 39928 ÷ 10 = 3992.8

11–14 **6** A one is always the digit on the left of a decimal point in a number (refer to the place value grids shown on Paper 2 Q41–45), therefore the decimal will be after the 6 in the number each time.

11 **16.739**   12 **936.17**
13 **6.7139**   14 **9136.7**

15–19 Use multiplication tables to solve the first part and then estimate and try possible missing numbers.

15 **10** 6 × 4 = 24; 24 × 10 = 240
16 **5** 2 × 9 = 18; 18 × 5 = 90
17 **3** 8 × 2 = 16; 16 × 3 = 48
18 **8** 5 × 7 = 35; 35 × 8 = 280
19 **10** 1 hour = 60 mins, so 2 hours = 120 mins. 10 × 12 = 120.

20–22 Refer to Paper 4 Q40–42 on rounding.
20 **5000** The 8 in 4807 rounds up to 5000.
21 **4800** The 0 in 4807 rounds down to 4800.
22 **4810** The 7 in 4807 rounds up to 4810.
23–26 Convert the kg to g to make the calculations easier: 1 kilogram is the equivalent of 1000g, so $\frac{1}{2}$ kg is 500 g and $\frac{1}{4}$ kg is 250g.
23 **14.00** 100g × 10 = 1000g; £1.40 × 10 = £14.00.
24 **13.60** 250g × 4 = 1000g; £3.40 × 4 = £13.60.
25 **Jeff** Work out how much Omar would pay for 1000g (1kg) and compare this to the others: 500g × 2 = 1000g; £6.45 × 2 = £12.90. Jeff pays £14.00, which is the most.
26 **Omar**
27–34 Refer to Paper 4 Q19 –21 on factors.
27–28 **2, 13** 2 × 13 = 26
29–34 **2, 15, 3, 10, 5, 6** 2 × 15 = 30; 3 × 10 = 30; 5 × 6 = 30
35 **24** 7^2 = 7 × 7 = 49; 5^2 = 5 × 5 = 25; 49 – 25 = 24
36–38 Use the column multiplication method shown on Paper 10 Q48 to multiply the amounts by 3, then multiply by ten (refer to Paper 2 Q41–45 on how to multiply decimal numbers by powers of 10).
36 **32.70** £1.09 × 3 = £3.27; £3.27 × 10 = £32.70
37 **34.50** £1.15 × 3 = £3.45; £3.45 × 10 = £34.50
38 **33.60** £1.12 × 3 = £3.36; £3.36 × 10 = £33.60
39 **Shop A** £32.70 is less than £33.00.
40 **30** £33.00 – £32.70 = £0.30
41–46 **a, b, c, e, g, h** If a shape has a line of symmetry, the shapes on either side of the line will be identical.
47–50 Refer to Paper 1 Q9–18 on sequences.
47–48 **3.25, 3.5** The sequence is to add 0.25; 3 + 0.25 = 3.25; 3.25 + 0.25 = 3.5.
49–50 **1, $\frac{1}{2}$ or 0.5** The sequence is to divide by 2; 2 ÷ 2 = 1; 1 ÷ 2 = 0.5.

Paper 12 (pages 33–36)

1 **21** Add all the numbers in the Venn diagram; 7 + 2 + 9 + 3 = 21.
2 **9** Add the numbers in the circle for "white roses"; 7 + 2 = 9.
3 **11** Add the numbers in the circle for "scented roses"; 2 + 9 = 11.
4 **2** Find the number in the overlap of the circles for "white roses" and "scented roses".
5 **10** Add the numbers outside the circle for "scented roses"; 7 + 3 = 10.
6 **3** Find the number outside both circles.
7 **09:27 or 9.27 a.m.** 2 hours after departure it will be 08:53. Add on 7 minutes to get to 09:00; 34 – 7 = 27 mins, so add this on to 09:00 to get 09:27.

8–10 Refer to Paper 2 Q41–45 on how to multiply decimal numbers by powers of 10.
8 **36**

10s	ones	•	$\frac{1}{10}$	$\frac{1}{100}$
	0	•	3	6
3	6	•		

9 **83**

10s	ones	•	$\frac{1}{10}$	$\frac{1}{100}$
	0	•	8	3
8	3	•		

10 **0.72**

ones	•	$\frac{1}{10}$	$\frac{1}{100}$	$\frac{1}{1000}$	$\frac{1}{10,000}$
0	•	0	0	7	2
0	•	7	2		

11–12 Measure each line with a ruler. 1 cm represents 3m, so 2cm represents 2 × 3 = 6m, and so on. Refer to Paper 1 Q4–8 on area of a rectangle.
11 **72** 2 × 3 = 6 and 4 × 3 = 12; 6m × 12m = 72m²
12 **63** 21 m × 3m = 63 m²
13 **72** 1 paving slab covers 1 m².
14 **54** 2 × 3 = 6 and 3 × 3 = 9; 6m × 9m = 54 m²
15 **63**
16–17 Refer to Paper 2 Q24 on ratio. There are 3 carp to every 5 goldfish, so the ratio is 3:5. Add up the ratio numbers (3 + 5 = 8), then divide the answer into the number of fish (32 ÷ 8 = 4). Finally, multiply this number by the individual ratios.
16 **20** 4 × 5 = 20
17 **8** 4 × 3 = 12 carp; 20 – 12 = 8 goldfish
18–21 To change a fraction into a decimal, divide the numerator (top number) by the denominator (bottom number). Refer to Paper 2 Q41–45 on how to divide numbers by powers of 10.
18 **0.43** 43 ÷ 100 = 0.43
19 **0.13** 13 ÷ 100 = 0.13
20 **0.6** 60 ÷ 100 = 0.60
21 **0.07** 7 ÷ 100 = 0.07
22–23 Subtract 7 from 39 and divide the answer by 2: 39 – 7 = 32; 32 ÷ 2 = 16. Then add 7 to the answer: 16 + 7 = 23.
22 **23**   23 **16**
24–26 Refer to Paper 4 Q40–42 on rounding.
24 **12,000** The 1 (in the hundreds column) in 12 188 rounds down to 12 000.
25 **12,200** The 8 (in the tens column) in 12 188 rounds up to 12 200.
26 **12,190** The 8 (in the ones column) in 12 188 rounds up to 12 190.
27 **36** Find numbers divisible by 3 then see which of them is also divisible by 4; 36 ÷ 3 = 12; 36 ÷ 4 = 9.

28–31 Use your times tables for the sixes, sevens, eights and nines

28 **28** $4 \times 6 = 24$; $24 + 4 = 28$

29 **39** $4 \times 9 = 36$; $36 + 3 = 39$

30 **37** $5 \times 7 = 35$; $35 + 2 = 37$

31 **33** $4 \times 8 = 32$; $32 + 1 = 33$

32 **56** $9 \times 6 = 54$; $54 + 2 = 56$

$$\begin{array}{r} 6 \text{ remainder } 2 \\ 9\overline{\smash{\big)}5\ {}^5 6} \end{array}$$

33 **53** $6 \times 8 = 48$; $48 + 5 = 53$

$$\begin{array}{r} 8 \text{ remainder } 5 \\ 6\overline{\smash{\big)}5\ {}^5 3} \end{array}$$

34 **7** $59 - 3 = 56$; $56 \div 8 = 7$

$$\begin{array}{r} 7 \text{ remainder } 3 \\ 8\overline{\smash{\big)}5\ {}^5 9} \end{array}$$

35 **6** $47 - 5 = 42$; $42 \div 7 = 6$

$$\begin{array}{r} 6 \text{ remainder } 5 \\ 7\overline{\smash{\big)}4\ {}^4 7} \end{array}$$

36–39

 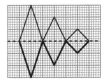

40 **5** $250 \div 58 = 4$ remainder 18, so 5 are needed but one will not be full. Refer to Paper 5 Q46 on long division or use repeated addition: $58 + 58 + 58 + 58 = 232$.

41–46 To change a fraction into a percentage, find the equivalent fraction with a denominator (bottom number) of 100. Make sure both numbers in the fraction are multiplied by the same number when doing this. The numerator (top number) in the fraction will be the same as the percentage.

41 **30** Multiply numerator and denominator by 10; $\frac{3}{10} = \frac{30}{100}$, which is 30%.

42 **40** Multiply numerator and denominator by 4; $\frac{10}{25} = \frac{40}{100}$, which is 40%.

43 **60** Multiply numerator and denominator by 5; $\frac{12}{20} = \frac{60}{100}$, which is 60%.

44 **60** Multiply numerator and denominator by 2; $\frac{30}{50} = \frac{60}{100}$, which is 60%.

45 **30** Multiply numerator and denominator by 2; $\frac{15}{50} = \frac{30}{100}$, which is 30%.

46 **70** Multiply numerator and denominator by 2; $\frac{35}{50} = \frac{70}{100}$, which is 70%.

47–50 Work from left to right. Refer to Paper 10 Q48 on column multiplication.

47 **123** $16 \times 8 = 128$; $128 - 5 = 123$

48 **163** $21 \times 8 = 168$; $168 - 5 = 163$

49 **307** $39 \times 8 = 312$; $312 - 5 = 307$

50 **331** $42 \times 8 = 336$; $336 - 5 = 331$

Paper 13 (pages 37–39)

1–3 Refer to Paper 9 Q29–35 on angles.

1 **32** $180° - 148° = 32°$

2 **233** $360° - 127° = 233°$

3 **52** $60° + 68° = 128°$; $180° - 128° = 52°$

4 **352** A total of 200 has been added on to the original numbers, so add 200 on to the answer: $152 + 200 = 352$.

5 **452** 300 has been added on to one of the original numbers, so add 300 on to the answer: $152 + 300 = 452$.

6 **652** A total of 500 has been added on to the original numbers, so add 500 on to the answer.

7 **5** Divide 135 by 3×9, that is divide by 3 then 9.

8 **5** Divide 200 by 4×10.

9–10 Refer to Paper 10 Q 50 on how to multiply decimal numbers.

9 **6.3**   10 **0.30**

11 **20,015** Refer to Paper 1 Q43 on writing large numbers using a place value grid.

12–15 Refer to Paper 1 Q4–8 on area and Paper 4 Q5 on perimeter.

12 **36 cm²** $12 \times 3 = 36$.

13 **30 cm** $12 + 3 + 12 + 3 = 30$.

14 **24 m** For a square, the length and width are the same; $6 \times 4 = 24$.

15 **36 m²** $6 \times 6 = 36$

16 **212** Rod sells sandwiches on 4 days; $4 \times 53 = 212$.

17 **4 h 20 min** Rod takes 65 minutes per day; 4×65 minutes or 4×1 h 5 min = 4h 20 minutes.

18–21 **30, 36, 42 and 48** Use the 6 times table.

22–24 **27, 36 and 45** Use the 9 times table.

25 **3** Multiply by 4, then by 3 to find what it will be times 12 (as $3 \times 4 = 12$) $250 \times 4 = 1000$; $1000 \times 3 = 3000$; 3000 m = 3 km

26 **4** $25 \times 4 = 100$; 100 cm = 1 m

27 $\frac{1}{2}$ **litre or 0.5 litre** $25 \times 10 = 250$; $250 \times 2 = 500$; 500 ml $= \frac{1}{2}$ litre

28–32 A pictogram uses pictures or symbols to represent information.

28 **10** 5 symbols represent 10 birds.

29 $\frac{1}{10}$ 24 symbols represent 48 birds; two $\frac{1}{2}$ symbols represent 1 bird each; $48 + 2 =$

EXPANDED ANSWERS

Bond Maths Assessment Papers 9–10 years Book 2

50 birds in total. $\frac{5}{50} = \frac{1}{10}$

30 **15** 7 symbols represent 14 birds; one $\frac{1}{2}$ symbol represents 1 bird; 14 + 1 = 15

31 **4** Chaffinches are represented with 6 symbols, which is 12 birds; pigeons are represented with 4 symbols, which is 8 birds. 12 − 8 = 4

32 **50**

33 **12:10** Noon on Friday is 5 days from noon on Sunday, so the clock will gain 2 × 5 = 10 minutes.

34–38 There are 360° in around a point. There are 8 compass points. 360 ÷ 8 = 45°.

34 **45**

36 **135** 45 × 3 = 135

35 **315** 360 − 45 = 315

37 **SE**

38 **E** 135° is 3 lots of 45

39 **180** 180° is half a turn.

40 **224** 32 × 7 = 224

41 **57** 399 ÷ 7 = 57

42–49 Measure each line with a ruler. 1 cm represents 5 m, so 2 cm represents 2 × 5 = 10 m, and so on. The area of a rectangle can be found by multiplying the length and width.

42 **15** 3 × 5 = 15

43 **60** 12 × 5 = 60

44–45 **20, 15** 4 × 5 = 20; 3 × 5 = 15

46–47 **40, 30** 20 m × 2 = 40 m; 15 m × 2 = 30 m

48–49 **8, 6** 40 ÷ 5 = 8; 30 ÷ 5 = 6

50 **10:49 a. m.** 7 minutes before 11:07 is 11:00; 11 minutes before 11:00 is 10:49.

Paper 14 (pages 40–42)

1–6 The horizontal axis shows the number of bedrooms and the vertical axis shows the number of houses that have that number of bedrooms.

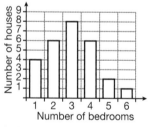

7 **3** The mode is the most frequent number: 8 houses have 3 bedrooms, which is more than any others.

8 **17** 8 + 6 + 2 + 1 = 17

9 $\frac{10}{27}$ The total of the houses is 27 (4 + 6 + 8 + 6 + 2 + 1 = 27); a total of 10 houses have 2 bedrooms or fewer (4 + 6); 10 out of 27 houses = $\frac{10}{27}$

10–11 Refer to Paper 1 Q19–24 on mixed numbers and improper fractions.

10 $1\frac{3}{10}$ 4 is the same as $\frac{40}{10}$ and $2\frac{7}{10}$ is $\frac{27}{10}$; $\frac{40}{10} - \frac{27}{10} = \frac{13}{10}$. As a mixed number this is: $1\frac{3}{10}$.

11 $2\frac{5}{7}$ 7 is the same as $\frac{49}{7}$ and $4\frac{2}{7}$ is $\frac{30}{7}$; $\frac{49}{7} - \frac{30}{7} = \frac{19}{7}$. As a mixed number this is $2\frac{5}{7}$

12 $1\frac{7}{10}$ There are $\frac{10}{10}$ in 1 whole; $\frac{10}{10} + \frac{7}{10} = \frac{17}{10}$, so $1\frac{7}{10}$

13 $1\frac{4}{5}$ There are $\frac{5}{5}$ in 1 whole; $\frac{5}{5} + \frac{4}{5} = \frac{9}{5}$, so $1\frac{4}{5}$

14 $2\frac{1}{3}$ There are $\frac{3}{3}$ in 1 whole, so $\frac{6}{3}$ in 2 wholes. $\frac{6}{3} + \frac{1}{3} = \frac{7}{3}$, so $2\frac{1}{3}$

15–16 This is partitioning. Refer to the place value grid in Paper 1 Q43 to help break the numbers down.

15 **90**

16 **3**

17 **9** Calculate the brackets first: 9 × 3 = 27; 27 + 9 = 36

18 **3** 4 × 5 = 20; 20 × 3 = 60

19 **5** 20 + 15 = 35; 7 × 5 = 35

20 **3** 8 + 5 = 13; 13 + 3 = 16

21–26 **1 and 32, 2 and 16, and 4 and 8** Refer to Paper 4 Q19–21 on factors.

27 **10** There are 31 days in October; 31 − 11 = 20; 20 ÷ 2 = 10

28 **15** 2 × 7 = 14; 58 ÷ 2 = 29; 29 − 14 = 15

29–33 **52 971, 79 315, 95 713.2, 297 135, 325 179** Refer to Paper 10 Q23–27 on ordering numbers.

34–39 There are 2 halves in a whole, so 4 halves in 2 wholes, 6 halves in 3 wholes and so on.

34 **9** 4 = 8 halves ($\frac{8}{2}$). Add this to the fraction in the mixed number to make $\frac{9}{2}$ ($\frac{8}{2} + \frac{1}{2} = \frac{9}{2}$). $\frac{9}{2}$ = 9 halves.

35 **12** 6 = $\frac{12}{2}$, so there are 12 halves.

36 **17** 8 = 16 halves. $\frac{16}{2} + \frac{1}{2} = \frac{17}{2}$, which is 17 halves.

37 **10** 5 = $\frac{10}{2}$, so there are 10 halves.

38 **19** 9 = 18 halves. $\frac{18}{2} + \frac{1}{2} = \frac{19}{2}$, which is 19 halves.

39 **23** 11 = 22 halves. $\frac{22}{2} + \frac{1}{2} = \frac{23}{2}$, which is 23 halves.

40 **21** 231 ÷ 11 = 21

41 **3.6** 4 × 0.9 = 3.6

42 **14** 43 − 29 = 14

43 **4** The ratio is 3:1, so add 3 litres of water to 1 litre of squash to find 4 litres.

44 **18** Write a list of the multiples of 6 and 9 and look for the lowest number in both lists: 2 × 9 = 18 and 3 × 6 = 18

45 **11:55** 12:00 is 2 hours 5 minutes before 14:10, so it started 5 minutes before 12:00.

46 **13:05** Count on from 11:55: 11:55 + 1hr = 12:55; 12:55 + 10 minutes = 13:05

47 **Regular** All angles equal and all sides equal.

48

Diagonals are lines from vertex to vertex.

49 **Pentagon or regular pentagon**

50 **44** 3.52 ÷ 8 = 0.44. Refer to Paper 3 Q30 on dividing into a decimal number.

A14

1–6 Refer to Paper 12 Q41–46 on converting fractions into percentages.

1 **50** Multiply the numerator and denominator by 5: $\frac{10}{20} = \frac{50}{100}$, which is 50%.

2 **20** Multiply the numerator and denominator by 2: $\frac{10}{50} = \frac{20}{100}$, which is 20%.

3 **60** Multiply the numerator and denominator by 5: $\frac{12}{20} = \frac{60}{100}$, which is 60%.

4 **85** Multiply the numerator and denominator by 5: $\frac{17}{20} = \frac{85}{100}$, which is 85%.

5 **40** Multiply the numerator and denominator by 4: $\frac{10}{25} = \frac{40}{100}$, which is 40%.

6 **66** Multiply the numerator and denominator by 2: $\frac{33}{50} = \frac{66}{100}$, which is 66%.

7 **5** A regular pentagon has 5 lines of symmetry.

8–9 Imagine the pentagon divided into 5 triangles.

8 $\frac{1}{5}$ 1 out of 5 triangles are grey.

9 $\frac{3}{5}$ 3 out of 5 triangles are black.

10 **60** Multiply the numerator and denominator by 20: $\frac{3}{5} = \frac{60}{100}$, which is 60%.

11 **20** $\frac{1}{5}$ of the pentagon is not white or black. $\frac{1}{5} = \frac{20}{100}$, which is 20%.

12–14 Refer to Paper 5 Q36–39 on plotting coordinates.

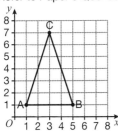

15 **Isosceles** Isosceles triangles have 2 equal sides and 2 equal angles.

16 **1** If a shape has a line of symmetry, the shapes on either side of the line will be identical.

17–21 A net is a 2-dimensional drawing of a 3-dimensional object. Imagine folding them. What 3-D objects do they make?

17 **No**   18 **Yes**
19 **Yes**   20 **No**
21 **No**

22–24 Refer to Paper 4 Q40–42 on rounding.

22 **6000** The 6 (hundreds) in 5636 rounds up to 6000.

23 **5600** The 3 in 5636 rounds down to 5600.

24 **5640** The 6 (ones) in 5636 rounds up to 5640.

25–30 This works like a ruler. Each division on the scale is 50 ml. A = 600 ml, B = 350 ml, C = 750 ml, D = 50 ml, E = 850 ml.

25 **250** 850 ml – 600 ml = 250 ml; or count on in 50s from A to E.

26 **250** 600 ml – 350 ml = 250 ml

27 **700** 750 ml – 50 ml = 700 ml

28 **500** 850 ml – 350 ml = 500 ml

29 **300** 350 ml – 50 ml = 300 ml

30 **150** 750 ml – 600 ml = 150 ml

31 **5788** Order the digits from smallest to largest.

32 **5321** Order the digits from largest to smallest.

33 **5321** They have the same number of thousands; 5788 has more hundreds than 5321.

34 **467** 5788 – 5321 = 467

35–39 Refer to Paper 1 Q19–24 on mixed numbers and improper fractions.

35 $\frac{7}{2}$ There are 6 halves in 3 wholes $\left(\frac{6}{2}\right)$. Add this to the $\frac{1}{2}$ in the mixed number to make $\frac{7}{2}$ $\left(\frac{6}{2} + \frac{1}{2} = \frac{7}{2}\right)$.

36 $\frac{21}{5}$ There are 20 fifths in 4 wholes $\left(\frac{20}{5}\right)$. Add this to the $\frac{1}{5}$ to make $\frac{21}{5}$ $\left(\frac{20}{5} + \frac{1}{5} = \frac{21}{5}\right)$.

37 $\frac{8}{3}$ There are 6 thirds in 2 wholes $\left(\frac{6}{3}\right)$. Add this to the $\frac{2}{3}$ to make $\frac{8}{3}$ $\left(\frac{6}{3} + \frac{2}{3} = \frac{8}{3}\right)$.

38 $\frac{11}{7}$ There are 7 sevenths in 1 whole $\left(\frac{7}{7}\right)$. Add this to the $\frac{4}{7}$ to make $\frac{11}{7}$ $\left(\frac{7}{7} + \frac{4}{7} = \frac{11}{7}\right)$.

39 $\frac{27}{5}$ There are 25 fifths in 5 wholes $\left(\frac{25}{5}\right)$. Add this to the $\frac{2}{5}$ to make $\frac{27}{5}$ $\left(\frac{25}{5} + \frac{2}{5} = \frac{27}{5}\right)$.

40 **$1\frac{3}{4}$** Remove the 1 from each of the numbers so you are left with the fraction only: $\frac{1}{2}$, $\frac{3}{4}$, $\frac{2}{5}$, $\frac{3}{8}$ and $\frac{3}{5}$. Change them into equivalent fractions with the same denominator: multiply the two largest denominators shown (5 and 8) together to find 40 and use this as a denominator. Multiply the numerator and denominator by the same number to change into equivalent fractions: $\frac{1}{2} = \frac{20}{40}$, $\frac{3}{4} = \frac{30}{40}$, $\frac{2}{5} = \frac{16}{40}$, $\frac{3}{8} = \frac{15}{40}$ and $\frac{3}{5} = \frac{24}{40}$. You will then be able to easily compare the fractions and see that $\frac{30}{40}$ is the largest, which is the equivalent of $\frac{3}{4}$, so the answer will be $1\frac{3}{4}$.

41–42 $\frac{4}{12}$, $\frac{6}{18}$ The sequence is to add 1 to the numerators and to add 3 to the denominators.

43 **9000** 9915 – 915 = 9000

44 **200** 5893 – 5693 = 200

45 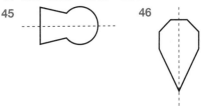   46

47–50 An easy way to add 99 is to add 100 and then subtract 1.

47 **375**   48 **933**
49 **485**   50 **602**

Paper 16 (pages 45–47)

1–9 Add the numbers in each of the columns. Refer to Paper 7 Q 9–12 on mode and range.

1 309
2 311
3 309
4 321
5 Jane The highest mark was Jane's, in English (86).
6 Stephen The lowest mark was Stephen's, in science (69).
7 10 82 – 72 = 10.
8 Melanie Jane: 86 – 71 = 15; Stephen: 84 – 69 = 15; Melanie: 85 – 78 = 7
9 79 79 occurs most often.

10–11 Add the numbers in each row to find the total for each subject; Maths 317; Science 307; English 326; History 300

10 English
11 History

12–16 Refer to Paper 2 Q41–45 on how to multiply numbers by powers of 10.

12 245
13 20.5
14 2450
15 20,450
16 245,000

17–23 The horizontal axis shows the day. The vertical axis shows how many newspapers were sold each day.

17 110
18 150
19 Saturday Look for the highest bar.
20 40 Friday shows 120 sold, Wednesday shows 80 sold: 120 – 80 = 40

21–22 Monday and Thursday Look for two bars that add to 150; 60 + 90 = 150
23 610 60 + 110 + 80 + 90 + 120 + 150 = 610
24 True 1550 > 1500
25 False 375 > 370
26 False 355 = 355
27 False 165.8 < 168.5

28–29 Refer to Paper 1 Q4–8 on area and Paper 11 Q10 on multiplying decimal numbers.
28 15.75 45 × 35 = 1575, so 4.5 × 3.5 = 15.75
29 6.75 27 ÷ 4 = 6.75
30 4361

```
    3  8  3  2
 +     5  2  9
 _____
    4  3  6  1
    1     1
```

31 56 If $\frac{1}{2}$ is 28 then double is 56.
32 20.2 Refer to Paper 4 Q 5 on perimeter. 5.7 + 5.7 + 4.4 + 4.4 = 20.2.
33 2.58
34 2.87

```
       2 . 5  8
 7 | 1  8 . 0  6
     1  4
     _____
        4    0
   -    3    5
     _____
        5    6
```

```
   ⁴5 . ¹⁶7 ¹2
 -  2 . 8  5
   _____
    2 . 8  7
           1
```

35 12.48

```
   5 . 9  6
   3 . 8  5
 + 2 . 6  7
 _____
 1 2 . 4  8
   2    1
```

36 22.96

```
      3 . 2  8
  ×         7
 _____
 2 2 . 9  6
      1    5
```

37–40 Use your multiplication tables.
37–38 32 ÷ 7, 28 ÷ 8 7 × 4 = 28; 28 + 4 = 32 and 8 × 4 = 24; 24 + 4 = 28
39–40 76 ÷ 8, 44 ÷ 5 8 × 9 = 72; 72 + 4 = 76 and 5 × 8 = 40; 40 + 4 = 44
41 718 350 × 2 is 700; 2 × 9 = 18; 700 + 18 = 718
42 £7.20 £3.50 × 2 is £7; 2 × 10p = 20p; £7.00 + 20p = £7.20
43 17 Refer to Paper 5 Q46 on long division or use the following method: 10 × 28 = 280 and 5 × 28 = 140 and 2 × 28 = 56
44 4 h 42 min Midnight to 4:37 is 4 h 37 min. The train left 5 minutes before midnight, so took 4 h 37 + 5 minutes.
45 0.34 or 34p 5.78 ÷ 17 = 0.34 Refer to Paper 5 Q46 on long division making sure the decimal point is aligned in the answer.
46 4.95 £9 ÷ 2 = £4.50; 90p ÷ 2 = 45p, so £4.50 + 45p = £4.95
47 $5\frac{3}{4}$ or 5.75 Half of 11 is $5\frac{1}{2}$ and half of $\frac{1}{2}$ is $\frac{1}{4}$, so $5\frac{1}{2} + \frac{1}{4} = 5\frac{3}{4}$
48–50 875, 625, 1000 $\frac{1}{4}$ of 2500 = 2500 ÷ 4, which is 625, so 625 are copper. 10% of 2500 = 250, so 40% = 250 × 4, which is 1000 so 1000 are zinc. 2500 – 625 – 1000 = 875 bent nails.

Paper 17 (pages 48–51)

1–7 The horizontal axis shows time and the vertical axis shows distance.
1 250 Look for the highest value.
2 200 3:00 p.m. is 15:00 in the 24-hour clock.
3–4 06:00, 09:00 The steepest line on the chart is between 06:00 and 09:00.
5–6 09:00, 03:00 Look along the gridline/y axis for 200 miles.
7 21.00 Look for the final point on the chart.
8 90 Even numbers are divisible by 2. The first number in this sequence will be 10. Count on in 2s. Add these numbers (10 + 12 + 14 + 16 + 18 + 20 = 90).
9–10 8, 4 Refer to Paper 4 Q5 on perimeter. The ratio is 1:2 (the width is half the length). Divide by 2 to get the combined measure of one width and one length: 24 ÷ 2 = 12. Add the ratio (1 + 2 = 3) and divide this into 12 (12 ÷ 3 = 4). Use the ratio of 1: 2 to find the width (1 × 4 = 4) and length (2 × 4 = 8).

11–13 Refer to Paper 5 Q25–28 on changing time into the 24-hour clock.

11 **20:30**   **12** **00:15**

13 **07:15**

14 **15** Round 39p to 40p to estimate: 40p x 15 is £6.00, so 15 can be bought.

15 **9712** Refer to Paper 2 Q35 on column subtraction. 10,000 – 288 = 9712

16 **0.9** 0.03 × 10 = 0.3; 0.3 × 3 = 0.9

17 **66** 60 × 1 = 60; 60 × 0.1 = 6; 60 + 6 = 66

18 **45** Divide 27 by 3 to find $\frac{1}{3}$: 27 ÷ 3 = 9 Then double 18: 18 × 2 = 36. Add the two numbers 9 + 36 = 45

19–21 Use the road map to find the distances and add the appropriate ones.

19 **32** 12 + 20 = 32   **20** **36** 20 + 16 = 36

21 **55** Via Burndale and Redridge it is 23 + 12 + 20 = 55; via Charwood it is 53 + 16 = 69

22 **Charwood** Charwood is 76 miles away via Ashbrook (23 + 53) and 48 miles away via Redridge and Purdek (12 + 20 + 16). You would reach each of these towns before reaching Charwood, so Charwood is the furthest away.

23 **60** 42 – 18 = 24; 18 × 2 = 36. Add the answers together to find the number of people: 24 + 36 = 60.

24–26 Refer to Paper 5 Q36–39 on plotting co-ordinates.

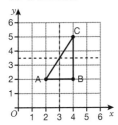

27 **0** If a shape has a line of symmetry, the shapes on either side of the line will be identical.

28 **B** A right angle is 90°

29–31 **5, 6, 9** Refer to Paper 4 Q27–30 on faces, edges and vertices.

32–34 **b, d, f** These are nets of 3-dimensional shapes. It is worth copying them to cut out and assemble to see which ones work and which ones do not.

35–40 Refer to Paper 1 Q9–18 on sequences.

35–36 **11, 11$\frac{1}{4}$** The sequence is to add $\frac{1}{4}$; $10\frac{3}{4} + \frac{1}{4} =$ 11; $11 + \frac{1}{4} = 11\frac{1}{4}$.

37–38 **0.635, 0.0635** The sequence is to divide by 10; 6.35 ÷ 10 = 0.635; 0.635 ÷ 10 = 0.0635. Refer to Paper 2 Q41–45 on how to multiply numbers by powers of 10.

39–40 **166, 155** The sequence is to subtract 11; 177 – 11 = 166; 166 – 11 = 155.

41 **8282**

```
    6 3 6 3
+   1 9 1 9
    8 2 8 2
      1       1
```

42 **14 616** Write the calculation again, swapping the positions of 36 and 406 and complete the sum as normal.

```
          4 0 6
    ×       3 6
        2 4 3 6
              3
+   1 2 1 8 0
            1
    1 4 6 1 6
              1
```

43 **58** Use long division (refer to Paper 5 Q46). Check your answer by multiplying it by 13.

44 **96.07** Refer to Paper 3 Q2 on column addition.

```
    8 3 . 0 4
    8 . 9 5
+     4 . 0 8
    9 6 . 0 7
    1   1     1
```

45 **27** To find $\frac{1}{10}$ of 30, divide 30 by 3: 30 ÷ 3 = 3; 30 – 3 = 27

46 **5** Count up in 25s to find the number closest to 120: 5 × 25 = 125.

47 **£9.95** Round £1.99 to £2.00: 5 × £2 = £10. This means 5 lots of 1p will have been added when rounding, so subtract them from the total to get the answer: £10 – £0.05 = £9.95

48 **174,000** 435 × 4 = 1740; 1740 × 100 = 174,000

49 **72** 110 – 38 = 72

50 **38.7**

```
            3 8 . 7
    8 | 3 0 9 . 6
    -   2 4
        6 9
      - 6 4
        5 6
```

Paper 18 (pages 51–54)

1–3 Refer to Paper 1 Q 4–8 on area.

1 **30** 6 × 5 = 30   **2** **6** 2 × 3 = 6

3 **9** The whole width of the gym is 5m and the bikes are 2m, so subtract this to find the width of the rowing machines: 3 × 3 = 9

4–13 Refer to Paper 4 Q19–21 on factors.

4–7 **1, 14, 2, 7** 1 × 14 = 14; 2 × 7 = 14

EXPANDED ANSWERS

Bond Maths Assessment Papers 9–10 years Book 2

8–13 **1, 28, 2, 14, 4, 7** 1 × 28 = 28; 2 × 14 = 28; 4 × 7 = 28

14 **30** 2 × 15 = 30   15 **60** 30 × 2 = 60

16–17 **15 and 30** Use your 3× and 5× tables.

18–19 **9 and 25** Use your 4× table. Look for numbers 1 more than the multiples of 4.

20–24 To change a fraction into a decimal, change it into an equivalent fraction with 10 or 100 as a denominator (bottom number). Then write the numerator (top number) in a place value grid (refer to Paper 2 Q21–23). Complete the reverse to change a decimal into a fraction. Refer to Paper 1 Q1–2 on reducing a fraction to its lowest terms.

20 **0.2** $\frac{1}{5} = \frac{2}{10}$; write the 2 in the tenths column to get 0.2

21 **0.7** Write the 7 in the tenths column to get 0.7

22 **0.11** Write 1 in the tenths column and 1 in the hundredths column to get 0.11

23 $\frac{3}{100}$ 0.03 = 3 hundredths, which is $\frac{3}{100}$

24 $\frac{3}{25}$ 0.12 = 12 hundredths, which is $\frac{12}{100}$. This can be simplified to $\frac{3}{25}$

25 **3.945** Remember to borrow where necessary. Refer to Paper 2 Q35 on column subtraction.

$$
\begin{array}{r}
^6 7 \ . \ ^{10}4 \ ^1 0 \ 9 \\
- \quad 3 \ . \ 1 \ 6 \ 4 \\
\hline
3 \ . \ 9 \ 4 \ 5
\end{array}
$$

26 **15.063** Ignore the decimal point when multiplying. Put the decimal point in the answer. There are 3 decimal places.

$$
\begin{array}{r}
5 \ . \ 0 \ 2 \ 1 \\
\times \qquad\quad 3 \\
\hline
1 \ 5 \ . \ 0 \ 6 \ 3
\end{array}
$$

27 **0.187**

$$
\begin{array}{r}
0 \ . \ 1 \ 8 \ 7 \\
7 \ \overline{) \ 1 \ . \ 3 \ 0 \ 9} \\
- \quad 7 \\
\hline
6 \ 0 \\
- \quad 5 \ 6 \\
\hline
4 \ 9
\end{array}
$$

28–31 Refer to Paper 8 Q5–10 on angles. A reflex angle is larger than 180° and smaller than 360°.

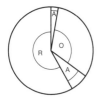

32–35 Carry out the calculations, then identify the matching pairs.

32 **26 × 3 = 156 ÷ 2** Both calculations give the answer of 78.

33 **80 – 14 = 6 × 11** Both calculations give the answer of 66.

34 **12 + 75 = 3 × 29** Both calculations give the answer of 87.

35 **63 ÷ 9 = 105 – 98** Both calculations give the answer of 7.

36 **5 books** Work this out using repeated addition: 5 lots of £3.60 = £18.00

37–38 **10, 5** Add all the numbers in the circle for "cats"; 4 + 2 + 3 + 1 = 10. Add all the numbers in the circle for "birds"; 3 + 1 + 1 + 0 = 5

39 **15** Add all the numbers in the Venn diagram; 2 + 2 + 2 + 3 + 0 + 4 + 1 + 1 = 15.

40 **12** Add the numbers in the circles for "cats" and "dogs"; 4 + 1 + 2 + 3 + 2 + 0 = 12.

41 **2** Find the number that is outside all of the circles.

42 **8.57 p.m.** 48 + 9 = 57

43 **40** 6² = 6 × 6 which is 36; 2² = 2 × 2 which is 4; 36 + 4 = 40

44 **113** 7² = 7 × 7 which is 49; 8² = 8 × 8 which is 64; 49 + 64 = 113

45 **9** 9² = 9 × 9 which is 81

46 **200** If $2 is equal to £1, multiply both numbers by 100 to find out how many Singaporean dollars there are for £100 (2 × 100 = 200).

47 **8500** If 85 rupees is equal to £1, multiply both numbers by 100 to find out how many Indian rupees there are for £100 (85 × 100 = 8500).

48 **5** If 130 rupees is equal to £1, divide 650 by 130 to find how many pounds there are (650 ÷ 130 = 5). Alternatively, count up in lots of 130 until you get to or near 650: 5 lots 130 is 650.

49 **300** If 70 baht is equal to £1, divide 21 000 by 70 to find how many pounds there are (21 000 ÷ 70 = 300). Alternatively, remove the zeros from both numbers and divide: 21 ÷ 7 = 3, so 21,000 ÷ 70 is 300.

50 **£3.20** If $\frac{3}{7}$ of his pocket money = £2.40, then $\frac{1}{7}$ = £2.40 ÷ 3 which is £0.80. $\frac{3}{7} + \frac{4}{7} = \frac{7}{7}$ (the total amount he receives). He spends $\frac{4}{7}$; £0.80 × 4 = £3.20.

Paper 19 (pages 54–57)

1–4 Refer to Paper 1 Q1–2 on reducing a fraction to its lowest terms and questions 19–24 on Improper Fractions and Mixed Numbers.

1 **5** There are 10 tenths in 1 whole $\left(\frac{10}{10}\right)$, so 20 tenths in 2 wholes $\left(\frac{20}{10}\right)$; $\frac{20}{10} + \frac{2}{10} = 2\frac{2}{10}$. $\frac{2}{10}$ can be reduced to $\frac{1}{5}$, so the mixed number is 2 wholes and $\frac{1}{5}$.

A18

2 **13** There are 3 thirds in 1 whole $\left(\frac{3}{3}\right)$, so 12 thirds in 4 wholes $\left(\frac{12}{3}\right)$. $\frac{12}{3} + \frac{1}{3} = \frac{13}{3}$.

3 **43** There are 7 sevenths in 1 whole $\left(\frac{7}{7}\right)$, so there are 42 sevenths in 6 wholes $\left(\frac{42}{7}\right)$. $\frac{42}{7} + \frac{1}{7} = \frac{43}{7}$.

4 **10** The denominator in the first fraction is 6 and in the second it is 3, so change it to an equivalent fraction first: $\frac{2}{3}$ is the same as $\frac{4}{6}$. There are 6 sixths in one whole $\left(\frac{6}{6}\right)$, so add this to $\frac{4}{6}$. $\frac{6}{6} + \frac{4}{6} = \frac{10}{6}$.

5 **<** 4 × 5 = 20; 19 + 3 = 22

6 **=** 9 − 7 = 2; 14 ÷ 7 = 2

7 **>** 12 ÷ 4 = 3; 3 − 1 = 2

8 **>** Follow the rules of BIDMAS and complete the equation in the brackets first: 3 + 10 = 13, so the calculation becomes: 2 × 13 = 26; 9 − 1 = 8, so the calculations becomes 3 × 8 = 24

9–12 The square has been separated into 8 rectangles of equal size, which means 1 rectangle is $\frac{1}{8}$. Refer to Paper 1 Q1–2 on reducing a fraction to its lowest terms.

9 $\frac{1}{4}$ 2 of the 8 rectangles are dotted. $\frac{2}{8} = \frac{1}{4}$.

10 $\frac{1}{8}$ 1 of the 8 rectangles is grey, which is $\frac{1}{8}$.

11 $\frac{3}{8}$ 2 rectangles are dotted and 1 is grey: $\frac{2}{8} + \frac{1}{8} = \frac{3}{8}$.

12 $\frac{1}{2}$ 2 rectangles have crosses and 2 have dots: $\frac{2}{8} + \frac{2}{8} = \frac{4}{8}$. This can be simplified to $\frac{1}{2}$.

13–14 **8 and 9** List he factors of 72 and look for 2 consecutive numbers: 1, 2, 4, 6, 8, 9, 12, 18, 36 and 72. 8 and 9 are the only consecutive numbers.

15 **6** The range is the difference between the highest and lowest numbers; 39 − 33 = 6.

16 **13.5** The ratio is 4 : 0.5. If there are 1.5 cups of cocoa, this is 3 times the ratio; multiply the 4 cups of flour by 3 to find an equivalent ratio of 12:1.5. Add these together to find the answer: 12 + 1.5 = 13.5.

17 **72** 2 × 36 = 72

18–20 Refer to Paper 2 Q41–45 on how to multiply numbers by powers of 10.

18 **32.20** If $3.22 is equal to £1, multiply both numbers by 10 to find out how many New Zealand dollars there are for £10 (3.22 × 10 = 32.20).

19 **28.67** If $2.867 is equal to £1, multiply both numbers by 10 to find out how many Australian dollars there are for £10 (2.867 × 10 = 28.67).

20 **171,200** If 17 120 rupiahs is equal to £1, multiply both numbers by 10 to find out how many Indonesian rupiahs there are for £10 (17,120 × 10 = 171,200).

21 **599,200** If 17 120 rupiahs is equal to £1, multiply both numbers by 35 to find out how many Indonesian rupiahs there are for £35 (17,120 × 35 = 599,200). Refer to Paper 3 Q1 on long multiplication.

22–25 The ruler is not drawn to scale. Each division on the scale is 0.1 cm. Will = 11.4 cm; Ashanti = 11.9 cm; Kate = 13.1 cm; Angie = 13.6 cm; Dan = 14.2 cm. Complete the answers as calculations or use the ruler to count to and from the numbers given.

22 **2.3** 14.2 − 11.9 = 2.3 (23 mm = 2.3 cm)

23 **2.8** 14.2 − 11.4 = 2.8 (28 mm = 2.8 cm)

24 **17** 13.1 − 11.4 = 1.7 (1.7 cm = 17 mm)

25 **17** 13.6 − 11.9 = 1.7 (1.7 cm = 17 mm)

26–31 To find equivalent fractions, multiply or divide the numerator and denominator by the same number.

26 **2** 5 × 5 = 25; 2 × 5 = 10

27 **21** 10 × 7 = 70; 3 × 7 = 21

28 **5** 6 × 7 = 42; 5 × 7 = 35

29 **20** 11 × 5 = 55; 4 × 5 = 20

30 **4** 9 × 6 = 54; 4 × 6 = 24

31 **35** 9 × 5 = 45; 7 × 5 = 35

32 **Fifty-five thousand and fifty** Refer to Paper 1 Q43 on writing large numbers using a place value grid.

33 **75** 9 × 8 = 72; 72 + 3 = 75

34–38 In each row, start with the time given and add or subtract to work out the other time or journey time. Count up to or back from the next hour to help avoid errors, remembering there are 60 minutes in one hour.

34 **08:40** 08:15 + 25 = 08:40

35 **10:35** 11.15 − 15 minutes = 11:00; 40 − 15 = 25, so count back a further 25 minutes from 11:00 to find 10:35.

36 **27** 57 minutes − 30 minutes = 27 minutes.

37 **13:20** 12:45 + 15 minutes = 13:00; 35 − 15 = 20, so count on a further 20 minutes to find 13:20.

38 **13:45** 14:30 − 30 minutes = 14:00; 45 − 30 = 15, so count back a further 15 minutes to find 13:45.

39–40 **3, 8** Refer to Paper 5 Q35 on finding the product. Write out the factor pairs of 24 and find the difference between each pair: 1 and 24, 2 and 12, 3 and 8, 4 and 6.

41 **36** 100% − 50% − 25% = 25% bronze. There are 9 bronze stickers, so 25% = 9. 4 × 25% = 100%, so 4 × 9 = 36 stickers.

42 **75** 90 minutes = $1\frac{1}{2}$ hours; the truck travels 50 km in 1 hour and 25 km in $\frac{1}{2}$ hour.

43–47 The horizontal axis shows the day. The vertical axis shows hours of sunshine.

43 **4** Look for points above the gridline for 5 hours

of sunshine. It may help to use a ruler or set square. It shone for more hours on Monday, Wednesday, Friday and Sunday.

44–45 **Tuesday and Saturday** Look for points below the gridline for 4 hours of sunshine. On Tuesday it shone for 3 hours; on Saturday it shone for 2 hours.

46 **43** Total the hours for all of the days; 10 + 3 + 8 + 5 + 8 + 2 + 7 = 43.

47 **19** 3 + 8 + 8 = 19

48–50 Refer to Paper 4 Q40–42 on rounding.

48 **2870** The 3 in 2873 rounds down to 2870.

49 **2900** The 7 in 2873 rounds up to 2900.

50 **3000** The 8 in 2873 rounds up to 3000.

Paper 20 (pages 57–59)

1 **3267** Refer to Paper 2 Q 35 on column subtraction or complete in the following way: 3300 − 30 = 3270; 3270 − 3 = 3267

2 **11** 15 + 7 = 22; 22 ÷ 2 = 11

3 **56** 42 ÷ 3 = 14; 14 × 4 = 56

4 **18** 3 eggs must be $\frac{1}{6}$ of the total; multiply by 3 to find $\frac{6}{6}$: 3 × 6 = 18.

5–8 Follow the rules of BIDMAS by completing the sum in the brackets first and use the inverse to help solve the equations.

5 **6** 5 × □ = 15 × 2 which is 30; 5 × 6 = 30.

6 **12** △ ÷ 3 = 8 − 4 = which is 4; 12 ÷ 3 = 4.

7 **5** 12 − ■ = 21 ÷ 3 which is 7; 12 − 5 = 7.

8 **13** 2 × ◇ = 21 + 5 which is 26; 2 × 13 = 26.

9–11 Use a ruler and a sharp pencil. Give your answers in mm.

9 **52**   10 **27**

11 **34**

12 **Acute** An acute angle is less than 90°.

13 **7212** Remember to borrow where necessary. Refer to Paper 2 Q35 on column subtraction.

```
  ⁷8  ⁹0  ¹⁰4  10
−      7    9    8
    7  2    1    2
```

14 **7940** As 397 is being multiplied by 20, write a 0 in the ones column for the answer and continue the calculations by multiplying the numbers by 2.

```
      3  9  7
×     2  0
   7  9  4  0
   ₁     ₁
```

15–20 There are 10 mm in a centimetre, 100 cm in a metre and 1000 m in a kilometre. There are 1000 ml in a litre and 1000 g in a kilogram. To convert from a smaller unit to a larger unit, multiply. To convert from a larger unit to a smaller unit, divide. Refer to Paper 2 Q41–45 on how to multiply numbers by powers of 10.

15 **0.4** 40 ÷ 100 = 0.4

16 **600** 0.6 × 1000 = 600

17 **0.5** 500 ÷ 1000 = 0.5

18 **52.6** 526 ÷ 10 = 52.6

19 **1640** 1.64 × 1000 = 1640

20 **1.8** 800 ÷ 1000 = 1.8

21–25

×	3	**6**	9
2	6	**12**	18
4	12	24	**36**
9	**27**	54	81

26 **55** Work in reverse: multiply 29 by 2 to get 58, then subtract 3 to get 55.

27 **16** 400m has been divided by 4 to get 100m; 1 minute 4 seconds = 64 seconds, so 64 ÷ 4 = 16

28 **33** 8:15 to 9:00 would be 45 minutes. Gayle arrives 12 minutes before 9:00; 45 − 12 = 33.

29–34

×	(3)	(7)	(11)
(5)	15	35	
(7)		49	77
(9)	27		99

35–40 Find the difference between 11:10 and the time shown.

35–36 **7, late** The time shown is 11:17; count on from 11:10 to 11:17 to find 7 minutes.

37–38 **14, early** The time shown is 10:56; count on from 10:56 to 11:10 to find 14 minutes.

39–40 **8, early** The time shown is 11:02; count on from 11:02 to 11:10 to find 8 minutes.

41–42 **90, 90** $\frac{3}{7}$ red, $\frac{1}{7}$ yellow, so orange must also be $\frac{3}{7}$ ($\frac{3}{7} + \frac{1}{7} + \frac{3}{7} = \frac{7}{7}$). Divide by 7 to find $\frac{1}{7}$: 210 ÷ 7 = 30; $\frac{3}{7}$ is 3 × 30 = 90.

43–47 The horizontal axis shows the day. The vertical axis shows the amount of water in the butt.

43–44 **Wednesday and Sunday** These are the only 2 days where the water level has risen.

45 **Thursday** The water level has dropped from Wednesday.

46 **20** It dropped from 50 to 30, which is 20.

47 **40** The lowest was 20, the highest 60; 60 − 20 = 40.

48 **240** Refer to Paper 10 Q15–20 on finding a percentage of a number. 10% of 600 is 60; 60% is 6 × 60 which is 360; 600 − 360 = 240

49 **$\frac{1}{6}$** $\frac{30}{30} - \frac{25}{30} = \frac{5}{30}$. Refer to Paper 1 Q1–2 on reducing a fraction to its lowest terms. $\frac{5}{30} = \frac{1}{6}$

50 **22** Refer to Paper 3 Q30 on short division. Alternatively, use the following method: 20 × 6 = 120; 2 × 6 = 12; 20 + 2 = 22.

1–2 Refer to Paper 20 Q15–20 on converting measures.

1 $\frac{1}{2}$**litre = 500 ml** 3.6m = 360cm; 360cm > 3.58 m

2 12 g > 0.01 kg

3–4 Refer to Paper 2 Q35 on using column subtraction. Alternatively, use the following methods.

3 3.9 4.6 – 0.6 = 4.0; 4.00 – 0.1 = 3.9

4 12.6 13.0 – 0.5 = 12.5; 12.5 + 0.1 = 12.6

5 7 Reverse the process. 3 × 3 = 9; 9 – 2 = 7.

6–7 12, 9 Add the 3 to 21 to get 24; 24 ÷ 2 = 12, which is Lila's age. Subtract 3 from 12 to get Charlie's age (9).

8 2 19 – 17 = 2

9–14 Refer to Paper 1 Q 4–8 on area and Paper 4 Q5 on perimeter.

	Side	Perimeter	Area
Square 1	9 cm	**36** cm	**81** cm²
Square 2	**7** m	**28** m	49 m²
Square 3	**6** mm	24 mm	**36** mm²

15 4 64 ÷ 16 = 4

16–17 Refer to Paper 7 Q 9–12 on mode and range.

16 11 The most frequent number is 11.

17 7 15 – 8 = 7.

18–20 To change a fraction into a decimal, divide the numerator (top number) by the denominator (bottom number). Refer to Paper 2 Q41–45 on how to divide numbers by powers of 10

18 0.21 21 ÷ 100 = 0.21

19 0.34 $\frac{17}{50} = \frac{34}{100}$; 34 ÷ 100 = 0.34

20 1.73 $\frac{100}{100}$ = 1, so subtract this from the fraction first $\left(\frac{173}{100} - \frac{100}{100} = \frac{73}{100}\right)$. 73 ÷ 100 = 0.73; 1 + 0.73 = 1.73.

21–29 Refer to Paper 4 Q27–30 on faces, edges and vertices.

	A	B	C
Number of faces	**Odd**	**Odd**	**Odd**
Number of vertices	**Odd**	**Even**	**Even**
Number of edges	**Even**	**Odd**	**Odd**

30 8.46 8.30 + 0.16

31 9.18 2 × 16 = 32: 8:36 + 32 minutes = 9:18.

32 9.50 Add on a further 32 minutes to 9:18 to get 9:50.

33 8.2 38mm is 3.8cm; 12 – 3.8 = 8.2

34 900 There are 60 seconds in a minute and 15 minutes in a quarter of an hour; 15 × 60 = 900.

35 19.829 7 litres + 12 litres = 19 litres; 329 ml + 500 ml = 829 ml, which is 0.829l. Add these totals together to find the answer: 19 + 0.829 = 19.829ml.

36–39 Tens are always the digit two places to the left of a decimal point in a number therefore the decimal will be two places after the 5 in the number each time. (Refer to the place value grids shown on Paper 2 Q41–45.)

36 56.413   **37 1356.4**

38 456.31   **39 31,456.0**

40 69 Refer to Paper 3 Q30 on using short division. 5.52 ÷ 8 = 0.69

41 4.48 Refer to Paper 2 Q35 on column subtraction. 10.00 – 5.52 = 4.48

42 3 1.5 kg = 1500 g, so he recycled 15 cans (1500 ÷ 100 = 15); 15 × 20p = 300p, which is £3.00

43–46 and 48–49 Refer to Paper 5 Q36–39 on plotting coordinates. Diagonals are lines between vertices inside the shape.

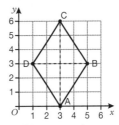

47 2 Obtuse angles are greater than 90° and less than 180°.

50 (3, 3) This is the point where the lines cross.

1 408 There are 24 hours in a day; 17 × 24 = 408. Refer to Paper 3 Q1 on long multiplication.

2–4 28, 35 and 42 Count up in your 7 times table from 4 × 7 (28), 5 × 7 (35) and 6 × 7 (42).

5–7 To find equivalent fractions, multiply or divide the numerator and denominator by the same number.

5 20 2 × 3 = 6; 2 × 10 = 20

6 9 $\frac{7}{7}$ = 1; $\frac{9}{9}$ = 1

7 10 $\frac{4}{8} = \frac{1}{2}$; $\frac{5}{10} = \frac{1}{2}$

8 14.64

```
    1 . 8 3
  ×       8
  1 4 . 6 4
      6   2
```

9 14,637

```
        6 9 7
  ×       2 1
        6 9 7
  + 1 3 9 4 0
      1   1
  1 4 6 3 7
    1   1
```

10 **760 r 8**

$$
\begin{array}{r}
7\ 6\ 0\ \ \text{r8} \\
1\ 2\ \overline{\big)\ 9\ 1\ 2\ 8} \\
-\ 8\ 4 \\
\hline
7\ 2 \\
-\ 7\ 2 \\
\hline
0\ 8 \\
\end{array}
$$

11 **Tonbridge** Look in the Midday column for the lowest figure.

12 **8** Range is the difference between highest and lowest; $10 - 2 = 8$.

13 **Liskeard** The coldest place is Moffat which was $-6°$, the next coldest place is Liskeard, which is $-3°$.

14 **Liskeard** Count up from $-3°$, through zero, to $10°$ to find $13°$ difference.

15–16 **Lampeter and Tonbridge** Freezing is $0°$ and neither of these temperatures is a minus value.

17–19 Count along the row once and return to the beginning to continue counting until you get to the number position you need.

17 □ There is a repeating pattern of 4 shapes: square, 2 circles, triangle, so every fourth shape will be a triangle. As the twelfth shape will be a triangle, the thirteenth shape will be a square.

18 □ There is a repeating pattern of 4 shapes: circle, rhombus, triangle, square, so every fourth shape will be a square, which means the twelfth shape will be a square.

19 ○ There is a repeating pattern of five shapes: 2 circles, triangle, 2 squares, so every fifth shape will be a square. As the fifteenth shape will be a square, the sixteenth and seventeenth shapes will be circles.

20 $2\frac{1}{4}$ Here are 4 quarters in 1 whole $\left(\frac{4}{4}\right)$, so 8 quarters in 2 wholes; $\frac{8}{4} + \frac{1}{4} = \frac{9}{4}$, so $2\frac{1}{4}$

21 $1\frac{3}{8}$ $11 \div 8 = 1$ r 3 There are 8 eighths in 1 whole $\left(\frac{8}{8}\right)$; $\frac{8}{8} + \frac{3}{8} = \frac{11}{8}$, so $1\frac{3}{8}$

22 $1\frac{1}{4}$ $5 \div 4 = 1$ r 1 There are 4 quarters in 1 whole $\left(\frac{4}{4}\right)$; $\frac{4}{4} + \frac{1}{4} = \frac{5}{4}$, so $1\frac{1}{4}$

23 $3\frac{1}{2}$ $7 \div 2 = 3$ r 1 There are 2 halves in 1 whole, so 6 halves in 3 wholes $\left(\frac{6}{2}\right)$; $\frac{6}{2} + \frac{1}{2} = \frac{7}{2}$, so $3\frac{1}{2}$

24 $1\frac{5}{6}$ $11 \div 6 = 1$ r 5 There are 6 sixths in 1 whole $\left(\frac{6}{6}\right)$; $\frac{6}{6} + \frac{5}{6} = \frac{11}{6}$, so $1\frac{5}{6}$

25 **5** $15 \div 3 = 5$ There are 3 thirds in 1 whole, so 15 thirds in 5 wholes.

26–27 **26, 13** Refer to Paper 4 Q 5 on perimeter. If the total perimeter is 78m, divide this by 2 to get the total length of one side and width of

one side: $78 \div 2 = 39$. The pool has a length twice as long as it is wide, so this is in a ratio of 2:1 (Refer to Paper 2 Q 24 on ratio). $2 + 1 = 3$, so divide 39 by 3 $(39 \div 3 = 13)$. Use the ratio of 2:1 to find the measurements: the length is 26 (2×13) and the width is 13 (1×13).

28–29 Ishmael owns 15 mice altogether, so the fractions will have 15 as a denominator. Fractions in their lowest form are also accepted.

28 $\frac{1}{5}$ or $\frac{3}{15}$

29 **60%** $\frac{9}{15} = \frac{3}{5}$. Find the equivalent fraction of $\frac{3}{5}$ with a denominator of 100 $\left(\frac{60}{100}\right)$; the numerator is the same number as the percentage (60%)

30 **16** $\frac{1}{9}$ of 36 is 4; $\frac{4}{9}$ is $4 \times 4 = 16$.

31–35 **3.52, 3.51, 3.25, 3.15, 3.05** Refer to Paper 10 Q23–27 on ordering decimal numbers.

36 **1418** The "Paris" column meets the "Rome" row at 1418

37 **London to Rome** London to Oslo is 1782 km; London to Rome is 1812 km.

38 **30** $1812 - 1782 = 30$

39 **1736** Rome to Manchester is 2156 km; Paris to London is 420 km; $2156 - 420 = 1736$.

40–41 Refer to Paper 2 Q41–45 on how to divide numbers by powers of 10.

40 **0.33** $\frac{33}{100}$ is the same as $33 \div 100$, which is 0.33

41 **0.54** $\frac{27}{50} = \frac{54}{100}$; $54 \div 100 = 0.54$

42–44 The total of hens and chicks is 1682. Subtract this from the total number of birds to find the amount of cockerels: $2224 - 1682 = 542$ cockerels. There are 1108 adult birds, so subtract the number of cockerels (542) from 1108 to find the number of hens: $1108 - 542 = 566$ hens. Subtract the number of hens (566) from 1682 to find the number of chicks: $1682 - 566 = 1116$ chicks.

42 **1116**   **43** **566**   **44** **542**

45 **11** Add 26 and 4 together and divide by 2 to find Eloise's age: $26 + 4 = 30$; $30 \div 2 = 15$. Subtract 4 from 15 to find Jean's age: $15 - 4 = 11$.

46–48 **26, 27, and 28.** Divide 81 by 3 to get the middle number: $81 \div 3 = 27$. To find the three consecutive numbers, include the numbers before and after 27.

49 **2.5** Refer to Paper 1 Q4–8 on area. $2.5 \times 1 = 2.5$.

50 **7** Refer to Paper 4 Q5 on perimeter; $2.5 + 2.5 + 1 + 1 = 7$.

Paper 23 (pages 65–67)

1–10 Refer to Paper 1 Q9–18 on sequences.

1–2 **12, 27** The sequence is to add 3; $9 + 3 = 12$; $24 + 3 = 27$.

3–4 **35, 17** The sequence is to subtract 6; 35 – 6 = 29; 23 – 6 = 17.

5–6 **7.5, 17.5** The sequence is to add 2.5; 5 + 2.5 = 7.5; 15 + 2.5 = 17.5.

7–8 **999, 0.0999** The sequence is to divide by 10; 999 ÷ 10 = 99.9; 0.999 ÷ 10 = 0.0999 Refer to Paper 2 Q41–45 on how to divide numbers by powers of 10.

9–10 **4, 36** This is the sequence of square numbers; $2^2 = 4$; $6^2 = 36$.

11 **0.39 or 39p** 1 kg costs £7.80 ÷ 5, which is £1.56; $\frac{1}{4}$ kg costs £1.56 ÷ 4, which is £0.39.

12 **13** 58 – 6 = 52; 52 ÷ 4 = 13

13 **26** 53 – 27 = 26

14 **1 h 17 min** Count up from 10:45 to the next hour: 10:45 to 11:00 is 15 mins. Count on another hour until 12:00, then add on the 2 minutes: 15mins + 1 hr + 2 mins = 1 hr 17mins

15 **1 h 40 min** 13:05 to 14:00 is 55 mins. Add on the 45 mins: 55 + 45 = 100 mins. There are 60 minutes in an hour, so subtract 60: 100 – 60 = 40 mins. This gives the answer 1hr 40 mins.

16 **Bus 1** Work out the time for Bus 3: 14:40 to 15:00 is 20 mins; 15:00 to 16:00 is 1hr. 16:00 to 16:01 is 1 min. 20mins + 1hr + 1 min = 1 hr 21 mins. Bus 1 completes the journey in the least amount of time.

17 **17** Bus 2: 13:26 to 14:00 is 34 mins; 14:00 to 14:45 is 45 mins. 34 + 45 = 79mins. Bus 3: 14:59 to 15:00 is 1 min; 15:00 to 16:00 is 60 mins; 16:00 to 16:01 is 1 min. 1 + 60 + 1 = 62 mins. 79 – 62 = 17 mins.

18 **3.89** Remember to borrow where necessary.

```
  ⁷8 .¹²3  ¹7
−  4 . 4  8
   3 . 8  9
```

19 **29.01** Remember to carry where necessary.

```
    1 6 . 2 9
 +  1 2 . 7 2
    2 9 . 0 1
        ₁   ₁
```

20 **3758.4**

```
        5 2 2
  ×       7 2
      1 0 4 4
 + 3 6 5 4 0
     ₁ ₁
   3 7 5 8 4
```

21 **307**

```
          3 0 7
  2 3 ⟌ 7 0 6 1
      − 6 9
          1 6 1
        − 1 6 1
```

22–25 Add or subtract the correct number of hours.

22 **7.00 p.m.** Islamabad is 5 hours ahead of London, so add 5 hours (2:00 + 5 hours = 7:00).

23 **8.00 p.m.** Los Angeles is 8 hours behind London, so add 8 hours (12:00 + 8 hours = 8:00).

24 **11.30 a.m.** Los Angeles is 8 hours behind London, so subtract 8 hours (7:30 – 8 hours = 11:30).

25 **6.30 p.m.** Los Angeles is 8 hours behind London, so add 8 hours (5:30 + 8 hours = 1:30 p.m.). Islamabad is 5 hours ahead of, so add 5 hours (1:30 + 5 hours = 6:30).

26–30 Refer to Paper 4 Q40–42 on rounding.

26 **48 100** The 2 in 48 126 rounds down to 48 100.

27 **39 100** The 5 in 39 057 rounds up to 39 100.

28 **29 300** The 9 (tens) in 29 292 rounds up to 29 300.

29 **53 400** The 4 (tens) in 53 444 rounds down to 53 400.

30 **89 100** The 8 (tens) in 89 089 rounds up to 89 100.

31 **4** 13 × 10 = 130; Divide 520 by 130 to find the third number: 520 ÷ 130 = 4.

32 **108** Odd numbers are not divisible by 2. The first number in this sequence will be 13. Count on in 2s and add the numbers together (13 + 15 + 17 + 19 + 21 + 23 = 108).

33 **100** 32 + 15 + 8 + 17 + 28 = 100

34 **Orange**

35 **15** 32 – 17 = 15

36–37 **Red and Orange** 100 cars = 100%, so look for 2 that add up to 40, which will be 40%. 32 + 8 = 40.

38–46 Refer to Paper 4 Q27–30 on faces, edges and vertices.

	A	B	C
Number of faces	6	8	4
Number of vertices	8	12	4
Number of edges	12	18	6

47–49 Refer to Paper 11 Q10 on multiplying decimal numbers together.

47 **0.311** After the decimals are removed the calculation becomes 933 ÷ 300; 933 ÷ 3 = 311; 311 ÷ 100 = 3.11. There are 3 decimal places in the original numbers, so there will be 3 decimal places in the answer: 0.311

48 **0.009** After the decimals are removed the calculation becomes: 3 × 3 × 1 = 9. There are 3 decimal places altogether in the original numbers, to there will be 3 decimal places in the answer: 0.009

49 **2.622**

50 **42** Refer to Paper 2 Q24 on ratio. There are 5 times as many oranges as there are lemons; 35 ÷ 5 = 7 lemons; 35 oranges + 7 lemons = 42 altogether.

Paper 24 (pages 67–70)

1–12 Refer to Paper 1 Q9–18 on sequences and Paper 1 Q1–2 on reducing a fraction to its lowest terms.

1–3 **21, 22, 25** The sequence is to alternate between adding 3 and adding 1; 18 + 3 = 21; 21 + 1 = 22; 22 + 3 = 25.

4–6 $\frac{3}{5}, \frac{1}{2}, \frac{2}{5}$ The sequence is to subtract $\frac{1}{10}$: the first, third and fifth fractions are tenths and the second, fourth and fifth are written in lowest terms; $\frac{7}{10} - \frac{1}{10} = \frac{6}{10}$; $\frac{6}{10} - \frac{1}{10} = \frac{5}{10}$, which is equivalent to $\frac{1}{2}$; $\frac{5}{10} - \frac{1}{10} = \frac{4}{10}$, which is equivalent to $\frac{2}{5}$.

7–9 **73, 63, 62** The sequence is to alternate between subtracting 1 and subtracting 10; 74 − 1 = 73; 73 − 10 = 63; 63 − 1 = 62.

10–12 **0.7, 0.9, 1.1** The sequence is to add 0.2; 0.5 + 0.2 = 0.7; 0.7 + 0.2 = 0.9; 0.9 + 0.2 = 1.1.

13 **Fourteen thousand, nine hundred and seventeen** Refer to Paper 1 Q43 on writing large numbers using a place value grid.

14 **18.96** Refer to Paper 4 Q 5 on perimeter. 6.5 + 6.5 + 2.98 + 2.98 = 18.96.

15 **3.84** Convert the numbers into the same type of measurement to complete the calculation: 480 cm − 96 cm = 384 cm or 4.80m − 0.96m.

16–20 Tenths are always the digit on the right of a decimal point in a number therefore the decimal will be to the left of the 3 in the number each time. (Refer to the place value grids shown on Paper 2 Q41–45),

16 **69.3** **17** **0.369** **18** **9.36**
19 **96.3** **20** **6.39**

21–26

×	(4)	(8)	(3)
(5)	20	40	
(6)		48	18
(9)	36		27

27 **10:23** 09:36 + 24 minutes = 10:00; 47 − 24 = 23, so count on a further 23 minutes; 10:00 + 23 minutes = 10:23

28 **11:49** 12:36 − 36 minutes = 12:00; 47 − 36 = 11 minutes, so count back a further 11 minutes to find 11:49.

29 **17:07** Add 11 minutes to 47 minutes to find a total of 58 minutes. 18:05 − 5 mins = 18:00; 58 mins − 5 mins = 53 mins; 18:00 − 53 mins = 17:07.

30 **8** $1 - \frac{1}{2} - \frac{1}{4} = \frac{1}{4}$, so $\frac{1}{4}$ is £2 which he spent on milk.; $\frac{1}{4} \times 4 = 1$ whole, so £2 × 4 = £8

31 **37** $\frac{1}{6}$ of 18 is 18 ÷ 6 = 3; 17 × 2 = 34; 3 + 34 = 37

32 **63** £45 − £9 = £36; 3 × £9 = £27; £27 + £36 = £63

33 **10** 5 × 8 = 40; 40 × 10 = 400

34 **50** 4 × 5 = 20; 20 × 50 = 1000

35 **20** 6 × 3 = 18; 18 × 20 = 360

36 **320** Move the decimal point to the right, the same number of places in each number, until you have two whole numbers (use the place value grid on Paper 2 Q41–45 to do this). Complete as normal and the answer will be the same: 2240 ÷ 7 = 320

37 **258** Add ones first. Ensure numbers are carried over if needed.

38 $\frac{1}{7}$ Refer to Paper 1 Q1–2 on reducing a fraction to its lowest terms. 18 + 3 = 21; $\frac{3}{21} = \frac{1}{7}$

39 **12:04** 11:51 to 12:00 is 9 minutes; 13 − 9 = 4 minutes; 12:00 + 4 minutes = 12:04

40–45 This is a horizontal bar chart. The longer the bar, the longer the time taken, so this will be the slower time.

40 **Petra** Look for the longest bar; 15 seconds is the slowest time.

41 **Jamelia** Look for the shortest bar; 9 seconds is the fastest time.

42 **Petra** Reading down the chart (May then June then July), Petra's bars get shorter.

43–44 Refer to Paper 7 Q9–12 on mode and range.

43 **6** 5 − 9 = 6.

44 **11** 11 occurs most often.

45 **Jamelia** Look for the shortest white bar, then the shortest grey bar and the shortest black bar.

46–50 Refer to Paper 1 Q1–2 on reducing a fraction to its lowest terms and Paper 12 Q41–46 on converting fractions into percentages. The regular octagon is divided into 8 equal sections, so the fractions will be eighths before being reduced $\left(\frac{1}{8}, \frac{2}{8}, \text{etc}\right)$.

46 $\frac{3}{8}$ 3 of the 8 triangles are covered with crosses. This cannot be reduced further.

47 $\frac{1}{2}$ 4 of the 8 triangles are either grey or dotted; $\frac{4}{8} = \frac{1}{2}$.

48 **25** 2 of the 8 triangles are grey; $\frac{2}{8} = \frac{1}{4} = \frac{25}{100}$; $\frac{2}{8} = \frac{1}{4}$ and $\frac{1}{4}$ is the equivalent of 25%.

49 **75** 6 of the 8 triangles are not dotted; $\frac{6}{8} = \frac{3}{4}$ and $\frac{3}{4}$ is the equivalent of 75%

50 **2** 50% is half, which would be 4 of the 8 triangles $\left(\frac{4}{8}\right)$; $\frac{2}{8} + \frac{2}{8} = \frac{4}{8}$.

EXPANDED ANSWERS

Bond Maths Assessment Papers 9–10 years Book 2

A24

The sum of two numbers is 39. The difference between them is 7.

22 What is the larger number? _____

23 What is the smaller number? _____

The volcanic mountain Teide on the island of Tenerife is 12 188 feet (3715 m) high. Give its approximate height:

24 to the nearest 1000 feet. _____ feet

25 to the nearest 100 feet. _____ feet

26 to the nearest 10 feet. _____ feet

Here is a set of numbers: 28, 36, 31, 39, 33, 37.

27 Which of these can be divided exactly by 3 and 4? _____

28 Which of these has a remainder of 4 when divided by 6? _____

29 Which of these has a remainder of 3 when divided by 9? _____

30 Which of these has a remainder of 2 when divided by 7? _____

31 Which of these has a remainder of 1 when divided by 8? _____

32–35 Write down the missing numbers.

$$9)\overline{}\quad 6 \text{ remainder } 2$$

$$6)\overline{}\quad 8 \text{ remainder } 5$$

$$8)\overline{59}\quad \underline{} \text{ remainder } 3$$

$$7)\overline{47}\quad \underline{} \text{ remainder } 5$$

36–39 Draw the reflections of these shapes in the mirror lines.

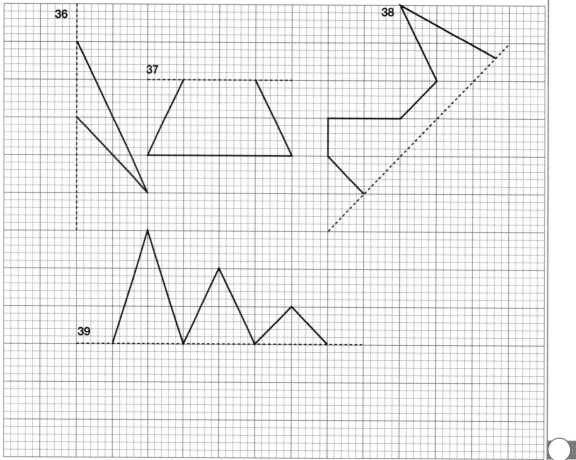

4

250 buns are to be packed into tins. Each tin holds 58 buns.

40 How many tins are required? _____

1

Write each of these fractions as a percentage.

41 $\frac{3}{10}$ _____ %   **42** $\frac{10}{25}$ _____%   **43** $\frac{12}{20}$ _____ %

44 $\frac{30}{50}$ _____ %   **45** $\frac{15}{50}$ _____ %   **46** $\frac{35}{50}$ _____ %

6

Write down the numbers that will come out of this machine.

47–50

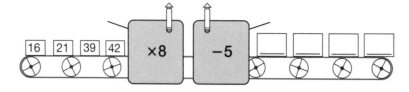

| 16 | 21 | 39 | 42 | ×8 | −5 |

4

Now go to the Progress Chart to record your score!   Total   50

Paper 13

Calculate the missing angles.

1

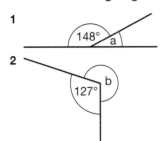

148° a

_____ °

2

127° b

_____ °

3

68°
60°
c

_____ °

Use this calculation to answer the questions.

```
   84
 + 68
  152
```

4   184
      + 168
      _____

5   384
      + 68
      _____

6   484
      + 168
      _____

Write down the missing numbers.

7 $3 \times 9 \times$ _____ $= 135$

8 $4 \times 10 \times$ _____ $= 200$

9 $3 \times 2.1 =$ _____

10 $5 \times 0.06 =$ _____

11 Write twenty thousand and fifteen in figures.   _____

Here is a list of measurements. For each question, choose the correct answer from this list.

24 cm   24 cm²   24 m   30 cm   30 cm²   30 m²   36 cm²   36 m   36 m²

12 What is the area of an envelope that is 12 cm long and 3 cm wide?   _____

13 What is the perimeter of the envelope?   _____

14 What is the perimeter of a square room that has sides of 6 m?   _____

15 What is the area of the square room?   _____

B 17

B 2

3

3

B 3

4

B 1

1

B 20

4

Rod sells sandwiches from Monday to Thursday. He sells 53 every day.

16 How many sandwiches does Rod sell in one week? _____

17 If it takes Rod 65 minutes to sell 53 sandwiches, how much
time does he spend selling them each week? _____ h _____ min

Write down all the numbers between 25 and 50 that are multiples of:

18–21 6 _____ , _____ , _____ and _____

22–24 9 _____ , _____ and _____

Write down the missing numbers.

25 250 m × 12 = _____ km

26 25 cm × _____ = 1 metre

27 25 ml × 20 = _____ litre

Here is a pictogram that shows the number of birds that visited the school bird table in one week.

Blackbird								
Blue tit								
Chaffinch								
Sparrow								
Pigeon								

Key: stands for 2 birds

28 How many blackbirds visited the bird table? _____

29 What fraction of the birds were sparrows? _____

30 How many blue tits visited the bird table? _____

31 How many more chaffinches visited than pigeons? _____

32 How many birds visited altogether? _____

33 The kitchen clock gains two minutes every day. If I put it right at noon on
Sunday what time will it show at noon the following Friday? _____

B 3
B 27
2
B 5
7
B 3
B 25
3
B 14
B 10
B 2
5
B 27
1

34 What is the size of the smaller angle between the arrow and S? _____ °

35 What is the size of the larger angle between the arrow and S? _____ °

36 What is the size of the smaller angle between the arrow and N? _____ °

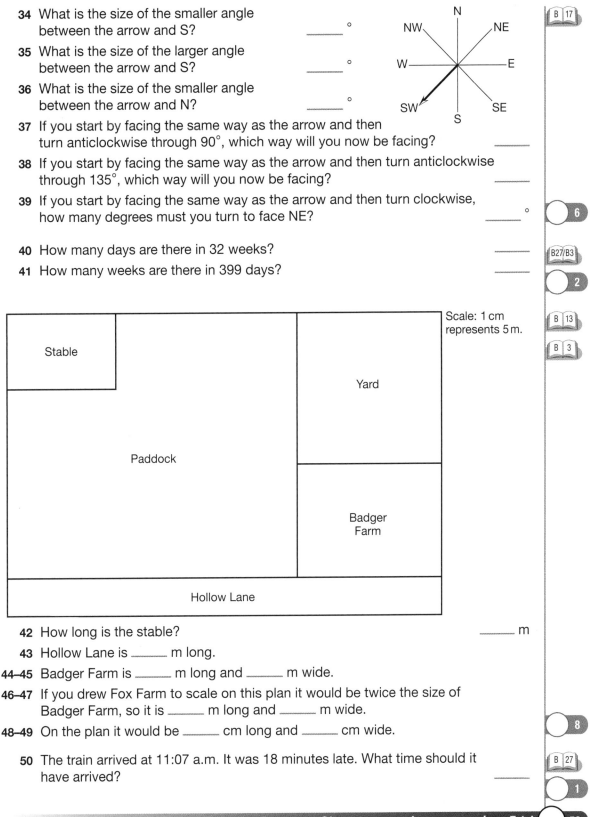

37 If you start by facing the same way as the arrow and then turn anticlockwise through 90°, which way will you now be facing? _____

38 If you start by facing the same way as the arrow and then turn anticlockwise through 135°, which way will you now be facing? _____

39 If you start by facing the same way as the arrow and then turn clockwise, how many degrees must you turn to face NE? _____ °

B 17

6

40 How many days are there in 32 weeks? _____

41 How many weeks are there in 399 days? _____

B27/B3

2

Scale: 1 cm represents 5 m.

Stable

Yard

Paddock

Badger Farm

Hollow Lane

B 13
B 3

42 How long is the stable? _____ m

43 Hollow Lane is _____ m long.

44–45 Badger Farm is _____ m long and _____ m wide.

46–47 If you drew Fox Farm to scale on this plan it would be twice the size of Badger Farm, so it is _____ m long and _____ m wide.

48–49 On the plan it would be _____ cm long and _____ cm wide.

8

50 The train arrived at 11:07 a.m. It was 18 minutes late. What time should it have arrived? _____

B 27

1

Now go to the Progress Chart to record your score! **Total** 50

39

Paper 14

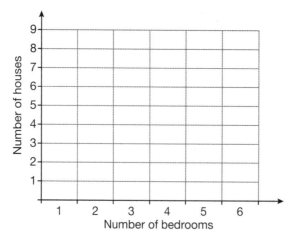

Number of houses (y-axis)
Number of bedrooms (x-axis)

1–6 Draw the bars on the chart above using the numbers from the table.

Number of bedrooms	Number of houses
1	4
2	6
3	8
4	6
5	2
6	1

7 What is the **mode** number of bedrooms?

8 How many houses have three bedrooms or more?

9 What fraction of the houses have two bedrooms or fewer?

Write down the missing numbers.

10 $4 - 2\frac{7}{10} =$

11 $7 - 4\frac{2}{7} =$

Write each of these **improper fractions** as a **mixed number**.

12 $\frac{17}{10}$

13 $\frac{9}{5}$

14 $\frac{7}{3}$

Write down the missing numbers.

15 $8396 = 8000 + 300 + \underline{\hphantom{000}} + 6$

16 $4173 = 4000 + 100 + 70 + \underline{\hphantom{000}}$

 B 14
 B 15
B 10

B 10
B 2
9

B 10
B 2
2

B 10
3

B 2
2

Write down the missing numbers.

17 $(9 \times 3) +$ _____ $= 36$

18 $4 \times 5 \times$ _____ $= 60$

19 $7 \times$ _____ $= 20 + 15$

20 $8 + 5 +$ _____ $= 16$

21–26 The pairs of **factors** of 32 are: _____ and _____ , _____ and _____ , and _____ and _____ .

27 October had 11 sunny days. Half the remaining days were rainy.
How many rainy days were there?   _____

28 Subtract twice 7 from half 58.   _____

Place these numbers in ascending order.

29–33 52 971   297 135   79 315   325 179   95 713.2

_____   _____   _____   _____   _____

Write down the number of halves in these numbers.

34 $4\frac{1}{2}$ _____

35 6 _____

36 $8\frac{1}{2}$ _____

37 5 _____

38 $9\frac{1}{2}$ _____

39 $11\frac{1}{2}$ _____

40 Work out how many times you can subtract 11 from 231.   _____

41 A square has sides that are 0.9 m long. What is the distance all the way
round the square?   _____ m

The sum of two numbers is 43.

42 If one number is 29, what is the other number?   _____

You need to add three parts of water to every one part of lemon squash.

43 How many litres of drink can be made with a litre of squash?   _____

44 What is the smallest number that can be divided by 9 and 6 without any
remainder?   _____

A tennis match lasted 2 hours and 15 minutes and ended at 14:10.

45 What time did the tennis match start? _____

46 The players had a break 1 hour and 5 minutes before the end of the game. What was the time? _____

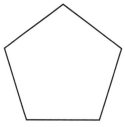

47 Is this **polygon** regular or irregular? _____

48 Draw all of the diagonals in the shape.

49 What is the shape you have made at the centre? _____

Divide a ribbon that is 3.52 m long into 8 equal pieces.

50 How long is each piece? _____ cm

Now go to the Progress Chart to record your score! **Total** ◯ 50

Paper 15

Write each of these fractions as a percentage.

1 $\frac{10}{20}$ = _____ %   **2** $\frac{10}{50}$ = _____ %   **3** $\frac{12}{20}$ = _____ %

4 $\frac{17}{20}$ = _____ %   **5** $\frac{10}{25}$ = _____ %   **6** $\frac{33}{50}$ = _____ %

Shape A 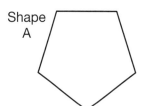   Shape B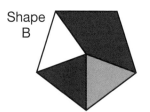

7 How many lines of symmetry does Shape A have? _____

8 What fraction of Shape B is grey? _____

9 What fraction of Shape B is black? _____

10 What is this fraction as a percentage? _____ %

11 What percentage of Shape B is not grey or black? _____ %

42

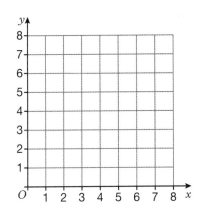

12–14 Plot and label the points A (1,1), B (5,1) and C (3,7). Join up the points.

15 What is the name of this sort of triangle? _____

16 How many lines of symmetry does it have? _____

5

Some of these nets make a cube. Write 'Yes' next to those that do, and 'No' next to those that don't.

17
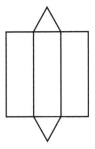 _____

18
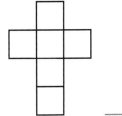 _____

19
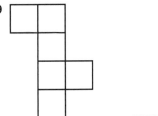 _____

20
 _____

21
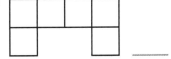 _____

5

Write 5636 to the nearest:

22 1000 _____

23 100 _____

24 10 _____

3

Look at this 1-litre jug.

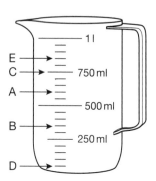

B 26

25 A to E measures   _____ ml

26 B to A measures   _____ ml

27 D to C measures   _____ ml

28 B to E measures   _____ ml

29 D to B measures   _____ ml

30 A to C measures   _____ ml   6

31 What is the smallest whole number that you can make with these digits?   B 1

    8   7   8   5   _____

32 What is the largest whole number that you can make with these digits?   B 1

    1   3   5   2   _____

33 Which of the answers to questions 31 and 32 is smaller?   _____   B 2

34 What is the difference between the answers to questions 31 and 32?   _____   B 2

   4

Write each of these **mixed numbers** as an **improper fraction**.   B 10

35 $3\frac{1}{2}$ _____   **36** $4\frac{1}{5}$ _____   **37** $2\frac{2}{3}$ _____

38 $1\frac{4}{7}$ _____   **39** $5\frac{2}{5}$ _____   5

40 Which of the following numbers has the highest value?   B 10

   $1\frac{1}{2}$ $1\frac{3}{4}$ $1\frac{2}{5}$ $1\frac{3}{8}$ $1\frac{3}{5}$ _____   1

41–42 Write down the missing fractions.   B 10

   $\frac{1}{3}$ $\frac{2}{6}$ $\frac{3}{9}$ _____ $\frac{5}{15}$ _____   2

What number needs to be added to or subtracted from: B 2

43 915 to turn it into 9915?   _____

44 5893 to turn it into 5693?   _____   2

Draw the lines of symmetry.

45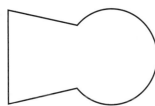

46

47 276 + 99 = _____

48 834 + 99 = _____

49 386 + 99 = _____

50 503 + 99 = _____

Now go to the Progress Chart to record your score! **Total** 50

Paper 16

	Jane	Jack	Stephen	Melanie
Maths	73	82	77	85
Science	79	80	69	79
English	86	77	84	79
History	71	72	79	78
TOTALS	_____	_____	_____	_____

1–4 Write each child's total in the table.

5 Who had the highest mark in any one exam? _____

6 Who had the lowest mark in any one exam? _____

7 What was the **range** of Jack's marks? _____

8 Who had the lowest **range** of marks? _____

9 What was the **mode** mark for all subjects? _____

10 In what subject was the highest total of marks gained? _____

11 In what subject was the lowest total of marks gained? _____

Multiply these numbers by 100.

12 2.45 _____

13 0.205 _____

14 24.5 _____

15 204.5 _____

16 2450 _____

Here is a bar chart that shows how many daily newspapers were sold by a newsagent over six days.

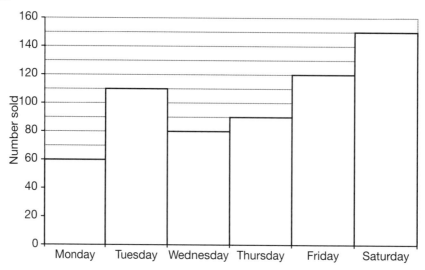

17 How many were sold on Tuesday? _____

18 How many were sold on Saturday? _____

19 On which day were the most newspapers sold? _____

20 How many more were sold on Friday than on Wednesday? _____

21–22 On which two days did the sales add up to Saturday's total? _____ and _____

23 How many newspapers were sold over the six days? _____

Write 'True' next to the statements that are true and 'False' next to those that are false.

24 $(155 \times 10) > (15 \times 100)$ _____

25 $(3.75 \times 100) < (37 \times 10)$ _____

26 $(35.5 \times 10) < (3.55 \times 100)$ _____

27 $(16.58 \times 10) > (1.685 \times 100)$ _____

28 What is the area of a carpet that measures 4.5 m $\times$ 3.5 m? _____ m^2

29 A rectangle has an area of 27 cm^2. Its width is 4 cm. What is its length?

_____ cm

30 Add five hundred and twenty-nine to three thousand, eight hundred and thirty-two. Write the answer in figures. _____

I ate half of my sweets and had 28 left.

31 How many did I have at the start? _____

32 What is the perimeter of a rectangle 5.7 cm long and 4.4 cm wide? _____ cm

33 _____
    7)18.06

34   5.72
      − 2.85
      _____

35   5.96
       3.85
     + 2.67
      _____

36   3.28
       ×   7
      _____

Circle the calculations that have a remainder of 4.

37–38 32 ÷ 7   33 ÷ 6   28 ÷ 8   31 ÷ 5

39–40 29 ÷ 3   76 ÷ 8   44 ÷ 5   41 ÷ 9

Double these values.

41 359 _____

42 £3.60 £ _____

43 Work out how many times you can subtract 28 from 476. _____

44 A train leaves at 11:55 p.m. on Friday and arrives at 4:37 a.m. on Saturday. How long does the journey take? _____ h _____ min

45 If £5.78 is shared equally among 17 people, how much does each person get? £ _____

Halve these values.

46 £9.90 £ _____

47 $11\frac{1}{2}$ kg _____ kg

My toolbox contains 2500 nails. $\frac{1}{4}$ are copper, 40% are zinc and the rest are bent.

48–50 I have _____ bent nails, _____ copper nails and _____ zinc nails.

Now go to the Progress Chart to record your score!   Total   50

47

Bodie drew a line graph to show the distance between himself and home on Tuesday.

B 14

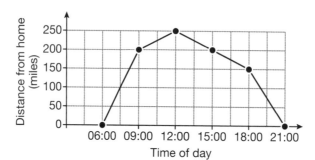

1 What was the furthest distance Bodie travelled from home? _____ miles

2 How far from home was he at 3:00 p.m.? _____ miles away

3–4 Between which two consecutive times did he travel the furthest? _____ and _____

5–6 Between _____ a.m. and _____ p.m. Bodie was 200 miles or more away from home.

7 What time did Bodie return home? _____

7

8 Add all the even numbers between 9 and 21. _____

B 2

1

9–10 A rectangle has a perimeter of 24 cm. It is half as wide as it is long.

It is _____ cm long and _____ cm wide.

B 20

2

Rewrite these times for a 24-hour clock.

B 27

11 Half past 8 in the evening. _____

12 Quarter past 12 in the morning. _____

13 Quarter past 7 in the morning. _____

3

14 How many 39p highlighters can be bought with £6.00? _____

B3/B2

15 Subtract two hundred and eighty-eight from ten thousand. _____

2

16 $30 \times 0.03 =$ _____

B 3

17 $60 \times 1.1 =$ _____

B 10

18 Add $\frac{1}{3}$ of 27 to twice 18. _____

3

48

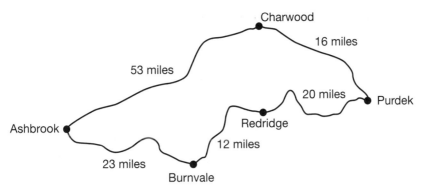

Charwood

16 miles

53 miles

20 miles Purdek

Redridge

Ashbrook

12 miles

23 miles

Burnvale

19 How far is it from Burnvale to Purdek via Redridge? _____ miles

20 What is the distance between Redridge and Charwood via Purdek? _____ miles

21 How long is the shortest route from Ashbrook to Purdek? _____ miles

22 What town is the furthest away by road from Burnvale? _____

4

23 There were 42 people at drama club. Eighteen left, but twice that number joined. How many are there now? _____

B3/B2
B 4
1

y

6
5
4
3
2
1

O 1 2 3 4 5 6 x

B 23
B 24
B 17

24 Plot and label the point A (2, 2).

25 Reflect this point in the vertical dashed line and label it B.

26 Reflect B in the horizontal dashed line and label it C. Join up A, B and C.

27 How many lines of symmetry does this shape have? _____

28 Which angle is a right angle: A, B or C? _____

5
B 21

29–31 This solid has _____ faces, _____ **vertices** and _____ edges.

3

B 2

32–34 Circle the three diagrams that are nets of the solid on the previous page.

a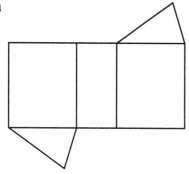

b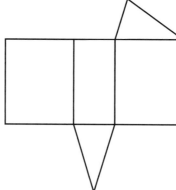

c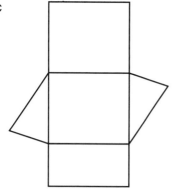

d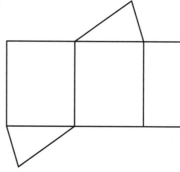

e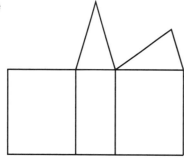

f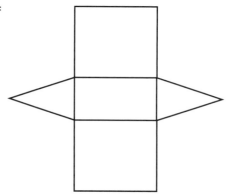

○ 3

Complete these sequences.

35–36 $10\frac{1}{4}$ $10\frac{1}{2}$ $10\frac{3}{4}$ _____   _____

37–38 635   63.5   6.35   _____   _____

39–40 188   177   _____   _____

○ 6

41	6363	42	36	43		44	83.04
	+ 1919		× 406		13)754		8.95
	_____		_____				+ 4.08

_____

○ 4

One-tenth of the cars in the car park are red. There are 30 cars altogether.

45 How many are not red? _____

There are 25 blank DVDs in a pack. Each pack of DVDs costs £1.99.

46 How many packs will you have to buy if you want 120 DVDs? _____

47 How much will you have to pay for 120 DVDs? £ _____

48 $435 \times 400 =$ _____

There were 110 people at a film. 38 left before the end.

49 How many watched the whole film? _____

50 Write the answer to this as a decimal.

$$8\overline{)309.6}$$

Now go to the Progress Chart to record your score! **Total** ◯ **50**

Paper 18

From this plan of a gym, calculate the areas used for each type of workout.

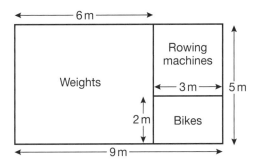

1 Weights = _____ m²

2 Bikes = _____ m²

3 Rowing machines = _____ m²

4–7 The pairs of **factors** of 14 are: _____ and _____, and _____ and _____.

8–13 The pairs of **factors** of 28 are: _____ and _____, _____ and _____, and _____ and _____.

(51)

Ravi completed 15 of his homework questions. Rochelle completed twice as many questions yet only managed to do half of the total questions.

14 How many questions did Rochelle complete? _____

15 How many questions were set for their homework? _____

| 3   12 |
| 1   9 |
| 15   6 |

| 7   20 |
| 2 |
| 25   30 |

For each of the questions, choose one number from each box.

16–17 Which numbers can be divided exactly by 5 and 3? _____ and _____

18–19 Which numbers have a remainder of 1 when divided by 4? _____ and _____

Write each of these fractions as a decimal.

20 $\frac{1}{5}$ _____

21 $\frac{7}{10}$ _____

22 $\frac{11}{100}$ _____

Write each of these decimals as a fraction in its **lowest term**.

23 0.03 _____

24 0.12 _____

25   7.109
       − 3.164
       _____

26   5.021
       ×   3
       _____

27   _____
       7)1.309

28–31 Label the **acute angles** 'A', the **obtuse angles** 'O' and the **reflex angles** 'R'.

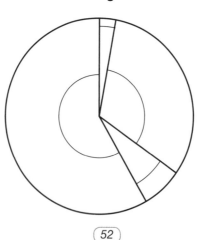

Match the calculations from list A with the ones from list B that have the same value.

B2/B3

List A   List B

26 × 3   105 − 98

80 − 14   3 × 29

12 + 75   156 ÷ 2

63 ÷ 9   6 × 11

32 _____ = _____

33 _____ = _____

34 _____ = _____

35 _____ = _____

4

36 If one book of stamps costs £3.60, how many books can you buy for £18.00? _____

B 3
1

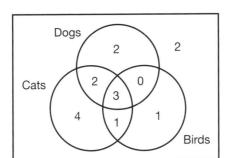

B 14

A vet has drawn this Venn diagram for all the pets owned by families living in his street.

37–38 _____ families own cats and _____ families own birds.

39 How many families live on the vet's street? _____

40 How many families own pets with four legs? _____

41 How many families do not have any pets? _____

5

42 A TV show started at 8:00 p.m. It lasted for 48 minutes and there were
9 minutes of advertising. When did the show finish? _____ p.m.

B 27
1

43 $6^2 + 2^2 =$ _____

44 $7^2 + 8^2 =$ _____

B2/B6

45 What is the square root of 81? _____

3

£1 = 85 Indian rupees
£1 = 2 Singaporean dollars
£1 = 130 Sri Lankan rupees
£1 = 70 Thai baht

46 How many Singaporean dollars can you get for £100? $ _____

47 How many Indian rupees can you get for £100?   _____ rupees

48 What are 650 Sri Lankan rupees worth in pounds?   £ _____

49 If you have 21 000 Thai baht, how many pounds can you get?   £ _____   ◯ 4

50 Randall saves $\frac{3}{7}$ of his pocket money every week. If he saves £2.40 each time, how much does he spend?   £ _____

B 10
B3/B2

◯ 1

Now go to the Progress Chart to record your score!   **Total** ◯ 50

Paper 19

Complete these changes of **improper fractions** to **mixed numbers**.

1 $\frac{22}{10} = 2\frac{1}{\underline{\hphantom{0}}}$ **2** $\frac{\overline{\hphantom{0}}}{3} = 4\frac{1}{3}$

3 $6\frac{1}{7} = \frac{\overline{\hphantom{0}}}{7}$ **4** $\frac{\overline{\hphantom{0}}}{6} = 1\frac{2}{3}$ ◯ 4

Write the correct sign, $<$, $>$ or $=$, in each space.

5 4×5 _____ $19 + 3$ **6** $9 - 7$ _____ $14 \div 7$

7 $12 \div 4$ _____ $3 - 1$ **8** $2 \times (3 + 10)$ _____ $3 \times (9 - 1)$ ◯ 4

A6/B3
B 2

What fraction of the square is:

9 dotted?   _____

10 grey?   _____

11 dotted or grey?   _____

12 covered in crosses or dots?   _____   ◯ 4

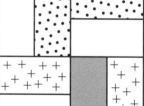

B 10

54

13–14 Two consecutive numbers multiply to 72. What are they?   _____ and _____   B6/B3

15 What is the **range** in this set of numbers?

33   37   39   37   38   _____

16 A cake mix uses 4 cups of flour for every half-cup of cocoa.
How many cups of cake mix can I make with 1.5 cups of cocoa?   _____ cups

17 What number is double 36?   _____

18 I have £10. How much money would
I have in New Zealand dollars? $ _____

19 How much is £10 in Australian
dollars? $ _____

£1 = 2.867 Australian dollars
£1 = 3.22 New Zealand dollars
£1 = 17 120 Indonesian rupiahs

20 How much is £10 in Indonesian rupiahs?   _____ rupiahs

21 How many rupiahs can I get for £35?   _____ rupiahs

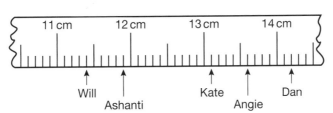

11 cm   12 cm   13 cm   14 cm

Will   Ashanti   Kate   Angie   Dan

Some children measured the length of their feet with a ruler and wrote down the results.

22 How much longer is Dan's foot than Ashanti's?   _____ cm

23 What is the difference between the longest and shortest feet?   _____ cm

24 How much shorter is Will's foot than Kate's?   _____ mm

25 What is the difference between Ashanti's foot and Angie's?   _____ mm

Complete these fractions.

26 $\dfrac{}{5} = \dfrac{10}{25}$

27 $\dfrac{3}{10} = \dfrac{}{70}$

28 $\dfrac{}{6} = \dfrac{35}{42}$

29 $\dfrac{4}{11} = \dfrac{}{55}$

30 $\dfrac{}{9} = \dfrac{24}{54}$

31 $\dfrac{7}{9} = \dfrac{}{45}$

32 Write out 55 050 in words.

_____

33 What number gives an answer of 8 remainder 3 when it is divided by 9? _____   B 3

34–38 Complete this table.   B 27

Buses leave at	Journey time	Buses arrive at
08:15	25 minutes	_____
_____	40 minutes	11:15
11:30	_____ minutes	11:57
12:45	35 minutes	_____
_____	45 minutes	14:30

5

39–40 The product of two numbers is 24. The difference between them is an odd number. The smaller number is _____ and the larger number is _____.   B 5

2

41 A teacher has a packet of star-shaped stickers. Fifty per cent are gold, 25% are silver and 9 are bronze. How many stickers does she have altogether? _____   B 12

1

42 How far will a truck going at a constant speed of 50 km/h (50 km in 1 hour) travel in 90 minutes? _____ km   B 3

1

Here is a line graph that shows the number of hours of sunshine in one week.   B 14

B 2

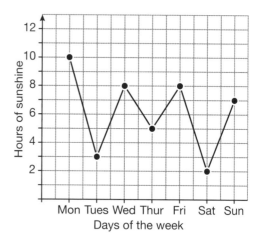

43 On how many days did the sun shine for more than 5 hours? _____

44–45 On which days did the sun shine for less than 4 hours? _____ and _____

46 How many hours of sunshine were there all week? _____ hours

47 How many hours of sunshine were there on Tuesday, Wednesday and Friday altogether? _____ hours

5

What is 2873 rounded to the nearest:

48 ten? _____

49 hundred? _____

50 thousand? _____

3

Now go to the Progress Chart to record your score! Total 50

Paper 20

1 What is the difference between 3300 and 33? _____ B2/B3

2 What number is halfway between 15 and 7? _____ B 10

3 If 3 times a number is 42, what is 4 times the number? _____

4 Jamal ate five-sixths of his Easter eggs in one day. If he has 3 left, how many did he start with? _____

4

What number does each symbol represent? B2/B3

5 $(5 \times \square) \div 2 = 15$ $\square =$ _____ B 8

6 $(\triangle \div 3) + 4 = 8$ $\triangle =$ _____

7 $(12 - \blacksquare) \times 3 = 21$ $\blacksquare =$ _____

8 $(2 \times \Diamond) - 5 = 21$ $\Diamond =$ _____

4

E •

• B

•
C

B 25

B 17

•
D

A •

9 Join A to C. How long is the line? _____ mm

10 Join B to D. How long is the line? _____ mm

11 Join E to B. How long is the line? _____ mm

12 Is angle DBE **acute**, **reflex** or **obtuse**? _____

4

13 8010
  − 798
  _____

14 397
  × 20
  _____

B2/B3

2

Write in the missing numbers.

15 _____ m = 40 cm   **16** 0.6 km = _____ m   **17** _____ litres = 500 ml

18 526 mm = _____ cm   **19** 1.64 km = _____ m   **20** _____ kg = 1800 g

21–25 Complete this multiplication table.

×	3	_____	9
2	6	_____	18
_____	12	24	_____
9	_____	54	81

26 Rose thinks of a number, adds 3 then divides by 2. The answer is 29.
What is Rose's number?   _____

27 Jared can run round his school's 400 m track in 1 minute 4 seconds.
How long would 100 m take if he ran at the same speed?   _____ seconds

28 Gayle left home at 8:15 a.m. and arrived at school at 12 minutes to 9.
How long did she take?   _____ minutes

29–34 Complete the brackets in this multiplication table.

×	(_____)	(_____)	(_____)
(_____)	15	35	
(_____)		49	77
(_____)	27		99

Imran sees the following three clocks just as the train due at 10 past 11 arrives at the station.

Decide if the train was early or late according to each clock. Write the number of minutes and circle the correct word.

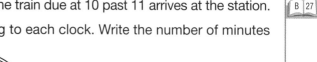

35–36 _____ minutes   early
                            late

37–38 _____ minutes early
late

39–40 _____ minutes early
late

6

41–42 In a flowerbed there are 210 tulips. $\frac{3}{7}$ of them are red, $\frac{1}{7}$ are yellow and the rest are orange. There are _____ red tulips and _____ orange tulips.

B 10
2

Here is a line graph that shows the amount of water in my garden water butt at the end of each day.

B 14
B 2

Days of the week

43–44 On which days did it rain?   _____ and _____

45 On which day did I use water from the water butt?   _____

46 How much water did I use?   _____ litres

47 What is the difference between the lowest and the highest level of water in the butt in the week?   _____ litres

5

48 A farm has 600 sheep. 60% of these are adults.

How many lambs are there?   _____

B 12
B 2
1

49 If 25 out of 30 cars passed their MOT tests, what fraction (in its **lowest term**) failed?   _____

B 10
1

50 Work out how many times you can subtract 6 from 132.   _____

B 3
1

Now go to the Progress Chart to record your score!   Total   50

Paper 21

Circle the true statements.

1 3.6 metres $<$ 358 cm

$\frac{1}{2}$ litre $=$ 500 ml

2 12 g $>$ 0.01 kg

45 minutes $> \frac{4}{5}$ hour

3 By how much is 4.6 greater than 0.7? _____

4 What is 13.1 minus 0.5? _____

5 Shari thinks of a number. If she adds 2 then divides by 3 the answer is 3. What is the number? _____

6–7 If you add Charlie's age to Lila's age it comes to 21 years. Lila is 3 years older than Charlie. Lila is _____ years old and Charlie is _____ years old.

8 The larger of two numbers is 19. The difference between them is 17. What is the smaller number? _____

9–14 Complete this table.

	Side	Perimeter	Area
Square 1	9 cm	_____ cm	_____ cm²
Square 2	_____ m	_____ m	49 m²
Square 3	_____ mm	24 mm	_____ mm²

15 How many 16 cm tall boxes can be stacked in a single column under a shelf 64 cm high? _____

16 What is the **mode** in this set of numbers?

17 11 13 15 18 18 11 9 7 11 12 11 14 _____

17 What is the **range** in this set of numbers?   13 8 12 15 _____

Circle the number that is equal to the fraction.

18 $\frac{21}{100}$ 2.1   2.01   0.021 0.21   21

19 $\frac{17}{50}$ 34   3.4   0.34   0.034 0.0034

20 $\frac{173}{100}$ 1.73   17.3   173   0.173 0.0173

B 10
B 11
3

A 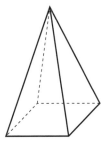   B 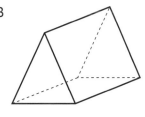   C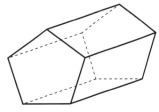

21–29 Complete the table, saying whether the number is odd or even for each shape.

B 21

	A	B	C
Number of faces			
Number of **vertices**			
Number of edges			

9

Eric should start at work at 8:30 a.m. He was 16 minutes late on Monday.

30 What time did he actually start work?   _____ a.m.

B 27

If he continues to be an extra 16 minutes late each day after that, at what time does he start work on:

31 Wednesday? _____ a.m   **32** Friday? _____ a.m

B 27
3

33 Subtract 38 mm from 12 cm.   _____ cm

B25/B2
1

34 How many seconds are there in a quarter of an hour?   _____

B 27
1

35 What is the sum of 7 litres, 329 ml and 12.5 litres?   _____ litres

B25/B2
1

Put a decimal point in each of the following numbers so that the 5 has a value of 50.

B 27

36 56413 _____   **37** 13564 _____

38 45631 _____   **39** 31456 _____

4

I bought 8 pens for £5.52. I paid using a £10 note.

40 How much did each pen cost? _____ p

41 How much change did I get? £ _____

42 My brother is paid 20p for every 100 g of cans he recycles. Last month he collected 1.5 kg. How much money was he paid? £ _____

43–46 Plot and label the points A (3,0), B (5,3), C (3,6) and D (1,3). Join up the points.

47 How many **obtuse angles** does this shape have? _____

48–49 Draw the lines of diagonals on this shape.

50 Circle the point that lies on both diagonals.

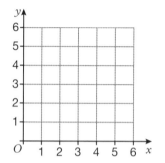

(0,0)   (4,3)   (2,4)   (3,3)   (5,3)

Now go to the Progress Chart to record your score!   Total   50

Paper 22

1 How many hours are there in 17 days? _____

2–4 Which numbers between 25 and 45 are exactly divisible by 7? _____ , _____ and _____

Complete these fractions.

5 $\dfrac{3}{10} = \dfrac{6}{\rule{1em}{0.4pt}}$

6 $\dfrac{7}{7} = \dfrac{\rule{1em}{0.4pt}}{9}$

7 $\dfrac{4}{8} = \dfrac{5}{\rule{1em}{0.4pt}}$

8 $\begin{array}{r} 1.83 \\ \times \quad 8 \\ \hline \end{array}$

9 $\begin{array}{r} 697 \\ \times \quad 21 \\ \hline \end{array}$

10   _____ r ___
$12\overline{)9128}$

Here is a table that shows the temperatures in different towns in Britain at midday and midnight on February 14th last year.

Town	Midday	Midnight
Moffat	3 °C	−6 °C
Swindon	5 °C	−1 °C
Lampeter	7 °C	4 °C
Liskeard	10 °C	−3 °C
Tonbridge	2 °C	3 °C

11 Where was the coldest place at midday? _____

12 What was the **range** of temperatures at midday? _____ °C

13 Where was the second coldest place at midnight? _____

14 Where was the biggest fall in temperature? _____

15–16 Which two places did not drop below freezing? _____ and _____

17 ☐○○△☐○○△   What will the 13th symbol be? _____

18 ○◇△☐○◇△☐   What will the 12th symbol be? _____

19 ○○△☐☐○○△☐☐   What will the 17th symbol be? _____

Write each of these **improper fractions** as a **mixed number**.

20 $\frac{9}{4} =$ _____

21 $\frac{11}{8} =$ _____

22 $\frac{5}{4} =$ _____

23 $\frac{7}{2} =$ _____

24 $\frac{11}{6} =$ _____

25 $\frac{15}{3} =$ _____

26–27 A swimming pool has a perimeter of 78 m. If it is twice as long as it is wide, its length is _____ m and its width is _____ m.

Ishmael owns 9 grey mice, 3 white mice and 3 brown mice.

28 What fraction of the mice are brown? _____

29 What percentage of the mice are grey? _____ %

30 There are 36 children in Charlotte's class. $\frac{4}{9}$ of the class are boys. How many boys are there? _____

Place these decimals in descending order.

31–35 3.15   3.05   3.51   3.25   3.52

_____   _____   _____   _____   _____

Distances are in kilometres.

London				
328	**Manchester**			
1782	2126	**Oslo**		
420	764	1791	**Paris**	
1812	2156	2591	1418	**Rome**

36 Jean-Pierre is driving with his family from Paris to Rome.
How far is that?   _____ km

37 Is it further from London to Oslo or from London to Rome? _____

38 What is the difference between these two distances?   _____ km

39 How much further is it from Rome to Manchester than from
Paris to London?   _____ km

Write each fraction as a decimal.

40 $\frac{33}{100}$ _____

41 $\frac{27}{50}$ _____

Remember: hens are adult female chickens. Cockerels are adult male chickens.

Arkvale Farm has 2224 chickens. There are 1108 adult birds and 1682 hens and chicks.

42 How many chicks are there?   _____

43 How many hens are there?   _____

44 How many cockerels are there?   _____

45 The ages of Jean and Eloise add up to 26 years. Jean is 4 years older than Eloise,
so Eloise is _____ years old.

46–48 Which three consecutive numbers add up to 81?   _____ , _____ and _____

A path is 2.5 m long and 1 m wide.

49 What is the area of this path?   _____ m²

50 What is the perimeter of this path?   _____ m

Now go to the Progress Chart to record your score!   Total   50

Complete these number sequences.

| 1–2 | 9 | _____ | 15 | 18 | 21 | 24 | _____ |

| 3–4 | _____ | 29 | 23 | _____ | 11 |

| 5–6 | 5 | _____ | 10 | 12.5 | 15 | _____ |

| 7–8 | _____ | 99.9 | 9.99 | 0.999 | _____ |

| 9–10 | 1 | _____ | 9 | 16 | 25 | _____ |

 B 7

 10

11 If 5 kilograms of cement cost £7.80, how much is $\frac{1}{4}$ kg?　　　　£ _____

B10/B3

1

12 What number am I thinking of, if the remainder is 6 when 4 times the number is taken from 58?　　　_____

B2/B3

1

13 The sum of two numbers is 53. The larger number is 27. What is the other number?　　　_____

B 2

1

Look at this timetable.

B 27

	Bus 1	**Bus 2**	**Bus 3**
Kingslea	10:45	13:05	14:40
Queensmead	10:59	13:26	14:59
Netherton	11:16	13:47	15:16
Middleton	11:33	14:10	15:33
Overton	12:02	14:45	16:01

14 How long does the first bus take to travel from Kingslea to Overton?　　　_____ h _____ min

15 How long does the next bus take to do the same trip?　　　_____ h _____ min

16 Which of the three buses does this journey the fastest?　　　_____

17 How much longer does the second bus take to travel from Queensmead to Overton than the third bus?　　　_____ minutes

 4

18	8.37	19	16.29	20	522	21	
	− 4.48		+ 12.72		× 7.2		23)7061
	_____		_____		_____		

B2/B3

 4

65

Islamabad is 5 hours ahead of London (+5 hours). Los Angeles is 8 hours behind London (−8 hours).

22 It is 2:00 p.m. in London. What time is it in Islamabad? _____

23 When it is noon in Los Angeles, what time is it in London? _____

24 When it is 7:30 p.m. in London, what time is it in Los Angeles? _____

25 What time is it in Islamabad when it is 5:30 a.m. in Los Angeles? _____

Round each of these numbers to the nearest 100.

26 48 126 _____

27 39 057 _____

28 29 292 _____

29 53 444 _____

30 89 089 _____

31 Three numbers are multiplied together to make 520. Two of the numbers are 13 and 10. What is the third number? _____

32 Add all the odd numbers between 12 and 24. _____

Here is a frequency table that shows the colours of cars that passed by Almond School in an hour.

Colour	Number of cars
Red	32
Yellow	15
Orange	8
Green	17
Blue	28

33 How many cars passed the school? _____

34 Which colour was seen the least? _____

35 How many more red cars were there than green? _____

36–37 Which two colours make up 40% of the cars? _____ and _____

66

38–46 Complete the table below for these solids.

A   B 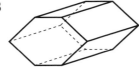 C

B 21

	A	**B**	**C**
Number of faces			
Number of **vertices**			
Number of edges			

 9

47 What is 93.3 divided by 300? _____

48 $0.3 \times 0.3 \times 0.1 =$ _____

49 What is 0.6 multiplied by 4.37? _____

B 11

 3

50 There are 35 oranges in a box. If there is 1 lemon in the box for every 5 oranges, how many oranges and lemons are there altogether? _____

B 13
B 4

 1

Now go to the Progress Chart to record your score!   Total   50

Paper 24

What are the next three terms in each of these number sequences?
Write fractions in the **lowest term**.

1–3 10   13   14   17   18   _____ _____ _____

4–6 $\frac{9}{10}$ $\frac{4}{5}$ $\frac{7}{10}$ _____ _____ _____

7–9 96   95   85   84   74   _____ _____ _____

10–12 0.1   0.3   0.5   _____ _____ _____

B7/B10

 12

13 Write out 14 917 in words.

_____

14 A rectangle is 6.5 cm long and 2.98 cm wide. What is its perimeter? _____ cm

15 Subtract 96 centimetres from 4.8 metres. _____ m

B 1
B 20
B2/B25

 3

Put a decimal point in each of the following numbers so that the 3 has a value of 3 tenths.

16 693 _____   **17** 369 _____   **18** 936 _____

19 963 _____   **20** 639 _____

21–26 Complete the brackets in this multiplication table.

×	(___)	(___)	(___)
(___)	20	40	
(___)		48	18
(___)	36		27

The local train takes 47 minutes to travel from Arkton to Biddlemere.

27 The 09:36 from Arkton arrives in Biddlemere at ____ : ____ .

28 The ____ : ____ from Arkton arrives in Biddlemere at 12:36.

29 Yesterday the train arrived in Biddlemere at 18:05. It was 11 minutes late.

What time did it leave Arkton?   ____ : ____

30 Janek spent half of his shopping money on bread, saved a quarter of it, and spent the rest on milk. If he spent £2 on milk, how much did he start with?   £ _____

31 Add $\frac{1}{6}$ of 18 to twice 17.   _____

32 Jonas has £45 in his bank account. He took out £9 and then put back three times as much as he took out. How much money does he have now?   £ _____

Write down the missing numbers.

33 $5 \times 8 \times$ _____ $= 400$ **34** $4 \times 5 \times$ _____ $= 1000$ **35** $6 \times 3 \times$ _____ $= 360$

36 Work out how many times you can subtract 0.07 from 22.4.   _____

B 1

5

B 3

6

B27/B2

3

B10/B2

1

B10/B2

B 3

1

B2/B3

1

B 3

3

B2/B3

B 11

1

37
```
  101
   14
   47
+  96
_____
```

38 In a class, 18 girls have long hair and 3 girls have short hair. What fraction (in the **lowest term**) of the girls have short hair? _____

39 A bus left Kirkwall Church at 11:51 and took 13 minutes to get to Stable Yard. When did it arrive? ___ : ___

Here is a bar graph that shows the race times for a 70 m sprint.

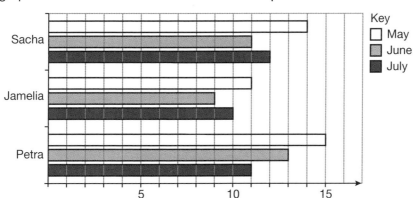

Key
☐ May
▨ June
■ July

Race times (seconds)

40 Who ran the slowest time? _____

41 Who ran the fastest time? _____

42 Who improved her time in every race? _____

43 What is the **range** of the race times? _____ seconds

44 What is the **mode** time for the 70 m sprint? _____ seconds

45 Who won every race? _____

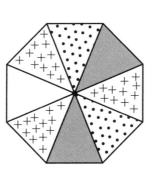

What fraction of the octagon (in **lowest terms**) is:

46 covered with crosses? _____

47 either grey or dotted? _____

48 What percentage of the octagon is grey? _____ %

49 What percentage of the octagon is not dotted? _____ %

50 How many more pieces would need to be dotted to cover 50% of the octagon? _____ ⑤

Now go to the Progress Chart to record your score!   Total ◯ 50

Progress Chart   Maths 9–10 years Book 2

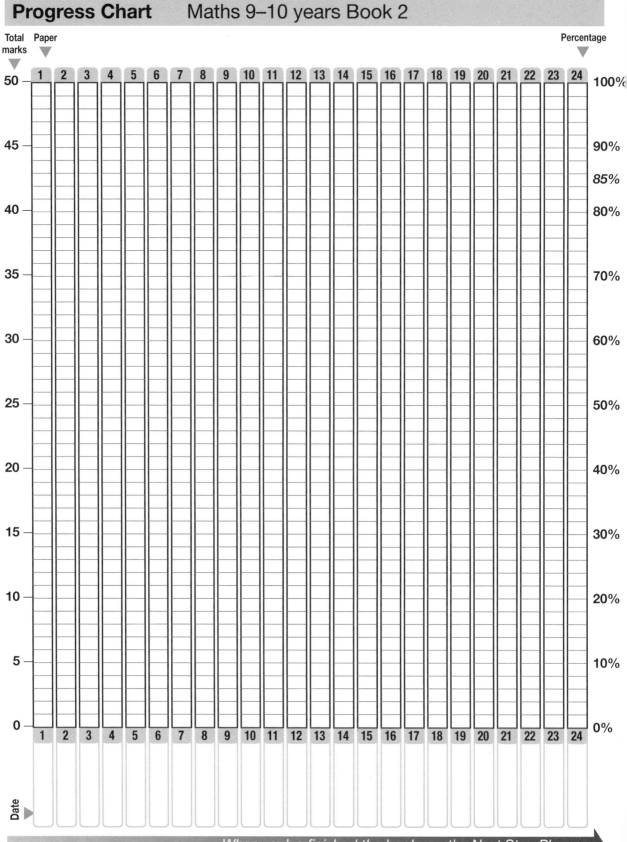

When you've finished the book use the Next Step Planner